Leonardo da Vinci

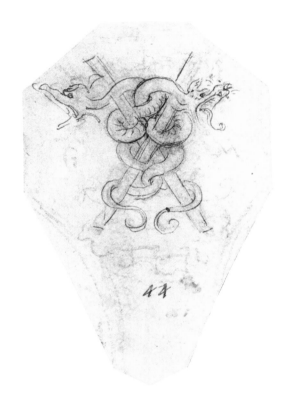

Leonardo da Vinci

A CURIOUS VISION

MARTIN CLAYTON

MERRELL HOLBERTON
PUBLISHERS LONDON

This catalogue accompanies an exhibition held at The Queen's Gallery, Buckingham Palace, 1 March 1996–12 January 1997. The drawings were selected by Martin Clayton and Jane Roberts. The author would like to thank Jane Roberts and Paul Joannides for their comments.

First published in 1996 by Merrell Holberton Publishers, Axe & Bottle Court, 70 Newcomen Street, London SE1 1YT

ISBN 1 85894 028 1

Produced by Merrell Holberton Publishers
Designed by Roger Davies
Typeset by SX Composing
Printed and bound in Italy by Grafiche Milani

Front jacket: *The head of Leda*, detail of cat. 40
Back jacket: *Studies of a woman's hands*, cat. 1

Half title: *An emblem of Galeazzo Maria Sforza*, cat. 28
Frontispiece: *A Star of Bethlehem, with crowsfoot and wood anemone*, cat. 41

Contents

Abbreviations

Throughout the catalogue the following abbreviations are used:

Briquet
Watermark numbers in C.M. Briquet, *Les Filigranes ...*, 3 vols., Paris 1907 (reprinted in 4 vols, Amsterdam 1968)

C.A.
Folio numbers in the Codex Atlanticus, Biblioteca Ambrosiana, Milan (see Further Reading)

MS.
Leonardo's notebooks in the Bibliothèque de l'Institut de France

P.
Catalogue numbers in A.E. Popham, *The Drawings of Leonardo da Vinci*, London 1946 and later editions

RL
Royal Library inventory numbers

A note on provenance

All the drawings and manuscripts in Leonardo's studio at his death were bequeathed to his favourite pupil Francesco Melzi, who took them back to his family villa near Milan. On Melzi's death, around 1570, the collection was sold by his son to the sculptor Pompeo Leoni, who attempted to arrange the loose material into some sort of order, often mutilating the sheets in the process. These sheets were pasted into the pages of several albums, of which two survive: the Codex Atlanticus, now in the Biblioteca Ambrosiana in Milan, and the volume that contained all the drawings now at Windsor (the binding has been preserved, as an empty shell).

The latter was auctioned after Leoni's death in Madrid in 1609, and somehow found its way to England; it was in the possession of Thomas Howard, Earl of Arundel, by 1630. During the Civil War, Arundel left England, and we have no idea of the whereabouts of the Leonardo volume until 1690, when it was recorded at Kensington Palace. The means by which the volume entered the Royal Collection is unknown.

The drawings were removed from the Windsor volume in the late nineteenth and early twentieth centuries, both for exhibition and to halt the abrasion of the chalk drawings, and solid-mounted on unsatisfactory board. In the early 1970s a programme of conservation was commenced, to lift all the Leonardo drawings from these mounts and encapsulate them between ultra-violet-filtered perspex sheets. Many of the drawings here are presented for the first time since the completion of this programme in 1992.

An outline of Leonardo's life

1452	15 April: Born at Anchiano, near Vinci, Tuscany
1469	Probably moves to Florence and enters the studio of Verrocchio
1472	Member of the Company of St Luke, Florence
ca. 1473–76	*Annunciation, Madonna with the carnation, Ginevra de' Benci*
1476	Still in Verrocchio's studio
1478	January: Commission for altarpiece for Palazzo della Signoria
ca. 1478	Benois *Madonna*
1481	March: Commission for *Adoration of Magi*
	September: Last payment for *Adoration of Magi*
ca. 1482	*St Jerome.* Moves to Milan
1483	April: Commission for *Virgin of the Rocks*
ca. 1483–89	Enters service of Ludovico Sforza. *Cecilia Gallerani, Portrait of a musician,* Louvre *Virgin of the Rocks*
1487–90	Architectural work in Milan and Pavia. First anatomical studies
ca. 1489–93	At work on Sforza monument
ca. 1494–97	At work on *Last Supper*; probably begins London version of *Virgin of the Rocks*
1498	Murals in Sala delle Asse, Castello Sforzesco, Milan
1499	December: Leaves Milan
1500	February: In Mantua. Portrait of Isabella d'Este
	March: In Venice, then to Florence
1501	April: At work on *Madonna of the Yarnwinder* and a cartoon of *Madonna and Child with St Anne*
1502–03	Architect, engineer and mapmaker to Cesare Borgia
1503	October: Begins cartoon of *Battle of Anghiari*
1504–05	At work on *Battle of Anghiari*; probably designs *Leda* and *Mona Lisa*
1505	Studies of birdflight and geometry
1506–07	Travelling repeatedly between Florence and Milan
1507–08	Winter: Dissection of centenarian in S. Maria Nuova, Florence
1508	Easter: Returns to Milan, in the service of Louis XII
1508–13	Studies of anatomy and water. Designs for Trivulzio monument. Probably begins panel of *Madonna and Child with St Anne*
1513	September: Leaves Milan
	December: In Rome, in the service of Giuliano de' Medici
1514–1516	Possibly at work on *Madonna and Child with St Anne, Mona Lisa, Leda, St John the Baptist*
1515	In Florence. Studies for new Medici Palace
1516	August: Last record in Rome
1517	January: At Romorantin, France
1517–19	In service of Francis I. Right hand paralysed. Architectural and geometrical studies. Designs for masquerades and equestrian monument. Assistants working on *Madonna and Child with St Anne*
1519	2 May: Dies at Amboise

The function and technique of Leonardo's drawings

The drawings by Leonardo that are connected directly with his artistic projects form only a small part of the surviving corpus. The remainder were his means of capturing form to record, comprehend and explain the infinite variety of experience, the theme of his whole career; for although Leonardo developed a rich and powerful literary style, he always maintained that an image transmitted knowledge more accurately and more concisely than any amount of verbiage. In Leonardo's drawings, therefore, we can follow a fertility and acuity of intellectual development seldom matched in the history of western thought.

Most of Leonardo's early sheets were little different in function from those of his contemporaries – a mixture of compositional sketches, studies of details for paintings, and drawing exercises. Yet from the first two qualities distinguish Leonardo's drawings, and are of great importance in understanding his works: his range of approach, and his obsessiveness. Leonardo's first datable drawing, a landscape study inscribed with the date 5 August 1473 (Uffizi, P. 253), records an intensely sympathetic response to natural processes; the sheet of profiles, cat. 5, shows observation subordinated to a pattern; by contrast, the studies of the bust of a woman, cat. 3, are completely extemporaneous. The last two drawings also display his obsessive streak, though the occasional impulse to fill a sheet with variations on a theme was sublimated in later life into a concentration on certain intellectual topics, such as the representation of deluges or the functioning of the valves of the heart.

The two principal drawing media of Leonardo's early years were metalpoint and pen and ink. Metalpoint makes use of the fact that when a metal stylus (usually made of silver) is drawn over the surface of a sheet of paper coated with a preparation of finely ground bone, it leaves an extremely thin layer of the metal which oxidizes immediately to give a dark-grey trace (this is distinct from leadpoint, a broad lead stylus used on untreated paper for underdrawing or coarse sketches). Varying the pressure on the stylus does not change the character of the line, and the mark cannot be erased. As the least capricious and most exacting medium, metalpoint demands control and discipline, and was thus the standard medium for the training of young artists in the studios of fifteenth-century Italy.

In Leonardo's early years he used metalpoint mainly for drawings from the life (cats. 1–3), and the more expressionistic pen and ink for sketches from the imagination (cat. 5). Brush drawing was usually ancillary, to wash in shadows or add white highlights, though a group of drapery studies that are associable with Leonardo and his peers are drawn solely with the brush on linen. The medium used for underdrawing is hard to identify with the naked eye both because of its inherent faintness and because of the rubbing the sheets have endured over the last five hundred years, but microscopic inspection at Windsor has shown that the underdrawing on Leonardo's earlier sheets is predominantly charcoal, not leadpoint.

It is impossible to construct a chronology of Leonardo's metalpoint drawings based on style alone, for their handling hardly evolves over the twenty years that he used the medium; datings must be based instead on motif and technique (see especially cat. 25). Leonardo's early pen-and-ink drawings are much more variable, and during the 1480s demonstrate a gradual taming of his vivaciously crude style, as his use of the pen became increasingly informed by the example of metalpoint. During the same period the distinction between the uses to which he put pen and metalpoint began to blur,

Detail of cat. 5

and by the late 1480s Leonardo had refined his control of the pen to such a degree that his drawings of the skull (cats. 20–21) display a sensitivity to surface modelling equalling that of his contemporary metalpoint studies of horses (cats. 24–25).

The 1480s also saw the functions of Leonardo's drawings diversify. Some time during the decade he entered the service of Ludovico Sforza, effective ruler of Milan, and for much of the rest of his life he was to earn his living through employment as a court artist, rather than by providing paintings to individual commission. Many of his subsequent drawings were made not for any immediate practical purpose, but as an investigation of form for its own sake or in the pursuit of knowledge in many guises, some of which may seem eccentric or even futile today. Initially he may consciously have emulated the Sienese artist, architect and engineer Francesco di Giorgio (1439–1501/02), who was in Milan at this time. Many of Leonardo's technical and architectural drawings were inspired by a manuscript in his possession that had been compiled by Francesco di Giorgio (Florence, Biblioteca Laurenziana); Francesco had initiated a treatise on architecture, and at this time Leonardo began to assemble material for a projected treatise on painting, an enterprise that he would never complete.

Around 1492–93 metalpoint was suddenly supplanted in Leonardo's drawings by red and black chalks, which over the next twenty years were to revolutionize draftsmanship in Italy. Black chalk had hitherto been used sporadically by northern Italian artists, especially for head studies, and had been available in Verrocchio's studio while Leonardo was working there in the 1470s. One sheet in red chalk by Leonardo (RL 12568) also appears to date from his early Florentine years, and is one of the earliest red-chalk drawings known. But it was only in the 1490s that Leonardo and other artists began to investigate the potential of chalk for a whole range of graphic effects.

At first, around 1492, Leonardo drew with red chalk in the manner of pen and ink, giving a spidery line that did little justice to the medium, and he used black chalk much as if it were charcoal, primarily for underdrawing. But he soon realised the tonal possibilities of both media, and in the *Last Supper* studies of the mid-1490s (cats. 29–31) his mastery of chalk is fully displayed. Over the next ten years black chalk was used by Leonardo in every way conceivable: for the most rapid small sketches (cat. 34), for heavily worked compositional studies (RL 12337), for smoky studies of form rubbed and accented with sharp lines (cat. 31), and for intricately modelled drawings using the point of the chalk only (the Budapest *Shouting warrior* for the *Battle of Anghiari*, P. 198, and, most probably, the lost presentation drawing of *Neptune* for Antonio Segni). By contrast, Leonardo soon restricted his use of red chalk to carefully modelled drawings, and rapid sketches such as cat. 36 are most unusual; being paler, red chalk has a narrower tonal range, though Leonardo stretched this to its limits with rubbing, stumping and washing (see cats. 29, 33, 61).

During the 1490s Leonardo began to use technically unnecessary coloured grounds. It was usual to tint the bone preparation of paper for metalpoint drawing, and in his youth Leonardo had employed some vivid orange, blue and purple grounds (cats. 2, 7). But his use of red prepared paper for red-chalk drawings from 1495 (cat. 29) can be ascribed only to an interest in the colouristic effects of the combination, which was to become one of Leonardo's favourite techniques in the following decade, and reached its logical – though sometimes illegible – conclusion in a group of drawings from the last years of his life executed in black chalk on dark-grey prepared paper (cat. 80).

Although the evidence is slight, it seems that no sooner had Leonardo mastered red and black chalks than he tried to expand the range of colours available by fabricating pastels in other colours. The one drawing in support of this assumption is the portrait of Isabella d'Este (Louvre, P. 172) of 1500, which employs a yellow pastel similar to that used by Clouet, Holbein and other northern portraitists a generation later. Lomazzo (1584) even credited Leonardo with the invention of the medium, though it had been used half a century earlier by French artists such as Fouquet.

This experimentation around 1500 set the tone for the last two decades of Leonardo's career, which were marked by a highly inventive manipulation of all available techniques. The combinations used were intelligent responses to certain pictorial challenges, not experiments for their own sake. Leonardo mixed black, red and occasionally white chalks on a red ground to give a richness to studies of hair (cats. 60, 61) or to atmospheric landscapes. The later drawings for the *St Anne* (cats. 78–80) are a culmination of the great technical attention that Leonardo had always paid to his drapery studies, which required the representation of both light and texture. Some of these studies, combining up to five media, are the most complex of all his drawings – cat. 78 employs layers of charcoal, black chalk, clear wash, brown wash and white heightening.

The use of black-chalk underdrawing for his scientific studies allowed Leonardo to mould the details into the most accurate configuration before committing himself to a definitive form in pen and ink; and in a number of scientific drawings from the years around 1510 he drew first with red chalk, and then reworked, outlined or refined the drawing with pen and ink. In the case of the water studies (cats. 65, 66) this use of red chalk was a means of achieving depth of structure on a flat sheet of paper. But the striking use of red in the embryological drawings (cat. 71) may be attributable instead to a desire, only partly conscious, to imbue these studies with something of the mystery of living flesh that distinguishes them from much of Leonardo's increasingly mechanistic anatomical work.

The scientific drawings, and particularly the anatomical studies, of Leonardo's later years are marked by a change in approach that mirrors the development of his philosophical system, evident in his notes. Before 1510, Leonardo's method had been to interpret what he saw in the light of what he knew (or what he thought he knew), recording this interpretation; the drawing was the end-product of his reasoning. After that date the drawing usually came first, and was the basis for his investigation of the functions of observed form. Leonardo's greatest skills were as an observer and a recorder, and thus, when his drawings were no longer limited by his imperfect knowledge, he produced some of the most

lucid and accurate anatomical illustrations in the history of science (cats. 67–69).

In the very last years of his life, Leonardo purged his drawings of much of their former colour, restricting his materials to black chalk and pen and ink, to the exclusion of red chalk. For a tinted ground he sometimes used a buff wash (cats. 79, 86, 87); occasionally, he would prepare the paper by rubbing black chalk into the surface, or by coating it with dark-grey bodycolour (cat. 80), producing a number of distinctive and somewhat disturbing black-on-black drawings. He used black chalk with greater subtlety than at any other time in his career: no artist ever attained the range of effect that Leonardo wrung out of the medium at the end of his life, in costume designs, equestrian studies and, in particular, depictions of deluges, immense and oppressive on a small scale and among the greatest drawings ever made.

We know from contemporary testimony that Leonardo lost the use of his right hand in his last years, and that he could therefore no longer paint (a two-handed operation); nor, by extension, could he have sculpted or made models. His drawings, made with his sound left hand, thus became the sole outlet for his ingenuity. In a way Leonardo ceased to be an artist. He became instead a visionary,

and his last drawings are those visions given as much materiality as the concepts could bear. The costume designs (cats. 88–93) may have been carried out by others, but no cloth could bring into existence the otherworldliness of those figures; indeed by being given a tangible form they would have been diminished, like a dream related after waking.

It is possible to see these last drawings as the logical conclusion of Leonardo's career. Throughout his life he had striven to realise the products of his imagination: occasionally he had succeeded, as in the *Mona Lisa* or the background of the *St Anne*; usually he had been thwarted, by events outside his control in the cases of the *Battle of Anghiari* and the Sforza monument, by his own flight from the extravagance of the *Adoration of the Magi*. Even the *Last Supper*, his greatest finished work, was deteriorating within his lifetime, for Leonardo had pushed his materials beyond the limits of their stability in an attempt to capture the effects he desired. Thus we can often grasp the true nature of Leonardo's intentions only through his drawings; and at the end of his life, when he had given up the unequal struggle to give large-scale form to his concepts, his drawings became the pure expression of his genius, boundless and magnificent.

1452–1481
Vinci and Florence

Detail of cat. 2

Leonardo was born on 15 April 1452 near the town of Vinci, fifteen miles west of Florence in the Arno valley. He was the illegitimate son of a peasant girl named Caterina and a young legal notary, Ser Piero da Vinci, and was taken into his paternal grandfather's house at an early age. Unusually for a great artist of the period, we have no idea of the nature of Leonardo's education, other than that he learned to read and write; as an illegitimate child, he was unable to follow his father's profession.

Vasari (1550) stated that Leonardo entered the workshop of Andrea del Verrocchio at an early age, but in 1469 he was still living in Vinci, with his paternal grandmother. Although Leonardo's presence in Verrocchio's studio is not documented until April 1476, when Leonardo was accused of sodomy (the charges were dismissed), the style of his first paintings would suggest that Leonardo entered the workshop as soon as he moved to Florence, after 1469. Yet by 1472, at the age of twenty, Leonardo had joined the painters' civic guild in Florence, the Company of St Luke; as this required full competence as a painter, either Leonardo had received a basic artistic training in Vinci, or he was a remarkably quick learner. Judging from his later career, the latter may have been the case, and for once Vasari's topos of the established master astonished by the drawings of the untutored youth may be no more than the truth.

The professional relationship between Verrocchio and Leonardo was more complicated than simply that of master and assistant, and Leonardo seems to have exercised his right as a member of the guild to accept contracts in his own name, while still putting his hand to workshop products: for the Uffizi *Annunciation*, the Munich *Madonna with the carnation* and the Washington portrait of *Ginevra de' Benci*, which are entirely by Leonardo, are all palpably earlier than his contribution (stylistically obvious and traditionally affirmed) to Verrocchio's Uffizi *Baptism of Christ*.

None of these early paintings is documented, and their dating is a matter of circumstantial evidence (see cat. 1) and stylistic analysis. The earliest project for which we have written records was an altarpiece of unspecified subject for the chapel of San Bernardo in the Palazzo della Signoria, commissioned in January 1478; in March that year Leonardo received a first payment for the painting, but we hear no more. There are also a number of drawings that have been claimed as studies for a painting of the *Adoration of the Shepherds*, though these are more probably Leonardo's first thoughts for the *Adoration of the Magi* (see cats. 6–9).

A fragmentary note on a drawing in the Uffizi (P. 127) records, "[...]ber 1478 I began the 2 Virgin Marys". The identity of these Madonnas is not known with certainty, and the two early paintings of the Madonna and Child by Leonardo that do survive – the Munich *Madonna with the carnation* and the Benois *Madonna* in the Hermitage – cannot be contemporary. (The tiny Dreyfus *Madonna* in Washington appears to be by a colleague of Leonardo in Verrocchio's workshop.) While the Munich picture must date from some years before the Benois *Madonna*, being stylistically much closer to the Uffizi *Annunciation* and thus probably of around 1472–74, the Benois *Madonna* is what one would expect of a composition conceived and painted a couple of years before the *Adoration of the Magi*, and may well be one of the two Madonnas referred to in the 1478 note.

Four other Madonna compositions by Leonardo could be dated to the same period. A painting in the Hermitage, the

Madonna Litta, is not by Leonardo but must be after a prototype by him, for there is a drawing by Leonardo for the head of the Madonna in the Louvre (P. 19). There is an enchanting series of studies for a Madonna and Child with a cat (P. 8–14), of much the same date; a sheet in the British Museum (P. 15–16) has on one side studies for the Benois *Madonna*, and on the other a sketch of a seated Madonna holding out a flower which the Child tries to grasp; and cat. 5 has on its reverse a composition of the *Madonna and Child with the infant Baptist*. Any of these compositions could be connected with a painting begun in late 1478, perhaps alongside the Benois *Madonna*, but the evidence is far too fragmentary for us to be dogmatic.

The only firmly datable painting to survive from Leonardo's first Florentine period is the unfinished *Adoration of the Magi* (cats. 6–9), commissioned in March 1481 by the monks of San Donato a Scopeto outside Florence. Our last indication of his presence in Florence is the delivery of a barrel of wine as part payment for this work on 28 September 1481.

This summary has touched only on Leonardo's painted works in his first decade as an artist. As a member of the workshop of Italy's most progressive sculptor in the 1470s, it is inconceivable that the ambitious and inquisitive youth did not try his hand at sculpture, and various pieces have been proposed as by him. The attribution to Leonardo of a marble portrait of a lady holding flowers in the Bargello, Florence, rests largely on the resemblance of the hands to those drawn in cat. 1, but the style of the piece is not sufficiently different from those sculptures securely by Verrocchio to support an ascription to the younger artist. Indeed it is not known whether Leonardo ever practised as a marble sculptor, and Vasari's statement (1550) that, years later, the government of Florence had considered assigning to Leonardo the huge block that eventually became Michelangelo's *David* is otherwise unsubstantiated. But he certainly knew how to work in clay, for the enormous model of the horse for the Sforza monument of the early 1490s presented a fearsome technical challenge in itself, and we may examine works of the 1470s in this light; of a pair of small terracotta angels in the Louvre, probably models for Verrocchio's Forteguerri monument (though this has been disputed) and thus after 1476, that on the right, markedly distinct in its characterization, may well be by Leonardo.

There remains the question of Leonardo's early scientific interests. A few of his youthful sheets bear drawings of joints, gears, architectural elements and so on, but there is no indication that these studies were pursued systematically, or that he was in any way in advance of contemporary understanding of technical matters. Leonardo's attempts to be taken seriously as an engineer (in the widest sense) do not seem to predate the 1480s; during his early Florentine years he was predominantly an artist – an extravagantly gifted artist, but not the universal man with whom we equate the name Leonardo today.

1

Studies of a woman's hands

ca. 1475–76
Charcoal underdrawing, metalpoint with white
heightening on pale-buff prepared paper
215 x 150 mm (8½″ x 5⅞″)
No watermark
RL 12558

This beautiful drawing is not a study of
two hands held one above the other, but
rather is two separate studies of crossed
hands, each study concentrating on one
hand only. It is probably preparatory for
the hands in a portrait, almost certainly of
Ginevra de' Benci, in the National
Gallery of Art in Washington (fig. 1). The
sitter, porcelain-faced against the foil of a
spiky juniper bush (*ginevro* in old Italian),
is now only shoulder length, but a fragmentary painting of a wreath on the
reverse of the panel shows that the painting has been cut down, and originally
would have included the sitter's hands.

The right hand appears to be holding
something between thumb and fore-
finger. An adaptation of the painting by
Lorenzo di Credi (Metropolitan Museum, New York) portrays a woman
holding a ring; it has been implied that
the object held by Ginevra was also a
ring, threaded on to the black ribbon
around her neck, and that the portrait was
thus painted at the time of her marriage
in 1474, aged sixteen. But rings in portraiture did not necessarily denote marriage; they could signify devotion of a
more general nature, and Jennifer Fletcher
(1989) has shown that the wreath on the
back of the panel combines Ginevra's
juniper with a bay branch and a palm
frond, the device of Bernardo Bembo, the
Venetian humanist whose platonic love
for Ginevra was celebrated by contemporary poets. Even if the portrait was not
actually commissioned by Bembo, it
therefore seems necessary to date its in-
ception to one of his two embassies to

Fig. 1   Leonardo da Vinci, *Ginevra de' Benci*
Oil and tempera on panel, 38.8 x 36.7 cm (15¼″ x 14½″). Washington, National Gallery of Art

Florence, in 1475–76 and 1478–80.
Stylistic arguments about Leonardo's earlier work are hazardous, but the hermet-
ic painting style would suggest the earlier
period, further from the expansiveness of
his first securely datable painting, the
Adoration of the Magi of 1481 (cats. 6–9).

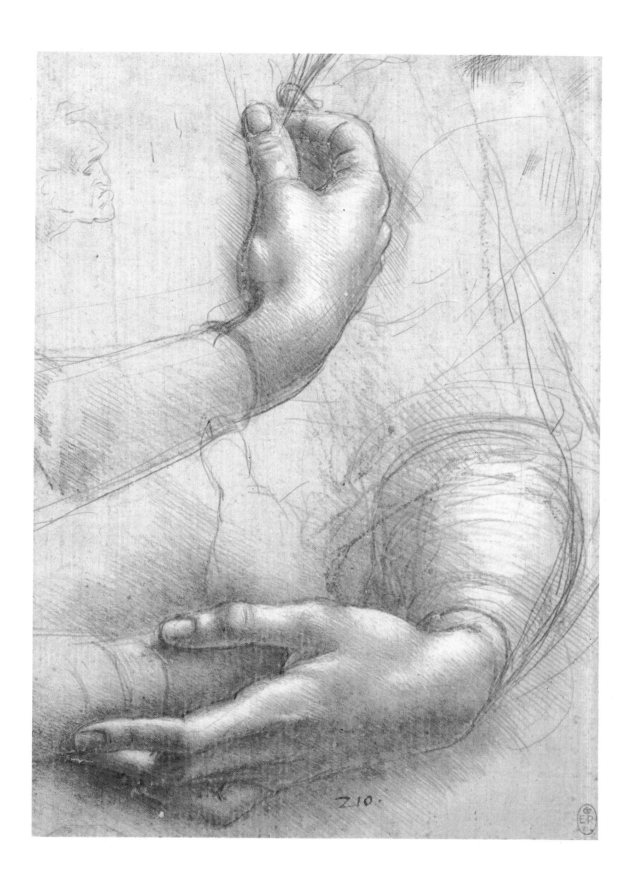

2

St John the Baptist

ca. 1475–78
Metalpoint with some white heightening on
blue prepared paper
178 x 122 mm (7″ x 4¹³⁄₁₆″)
No watermark
RL 12572

The long hair, reed cross and pointing
gesture of the youth identify this drawing
as a study for a figure of the Baptist; the
object at which he appears to point is a
second study for the top of the reed cross.
The technique is little different from the
horse and nude studies of around 1490
(cats. 25, 19), but the extremely slender
proportions of the figure indicate that the
drawing is a work of the 1470s. Some
time between 1474 and 1478 Verrocchio
and his assistants began work on an altarpiece of the *Madonna and Child enthroned
with Sts Donatus and John the Baptist*, still
in the Cathedral in Pistoia. But although
the Baptist in that painting (probably the
last part of the panel to be finished, by
Lorenzo di Credi) does bear some similarities in pose to that of the present figure, there he is a rugged ascetic staring
out at the spectator, here a langorous
youth, of the type favoured by Leonardo
throughout his career, peering coyly from
under half-closed eyelids.

It is tempting to describe any sheet
such as this – fully worked out in pose
and carefully drawn from the life – as a
study for a lost painting, and that may
well have been the case here: the Baptist
was one of the patron saints of Florence
and was very frequently depicted in the
city throughout the fifteenth century. On
the other hand artists invented poses, and
copied other drawings and paintings, for
future reference or simply to practise
their draftsmanship. Each artist would
have had a considerable stock of such
sheets, made with no immediate purpose,
but just as much tools of his trade as
brushes and pigments.

3

Studies of a woman, bust length

ca. 1478
Metalpoint on pale pinkish-buff prepared paper
232 x 190 mm (9⅛″ x 7½″)
No watermark
RL 12513

4

Studies of a baby

ca. 1478
Metalpoint, partly gone over with pen and ink,
on pale pinkish-buff prepared paper
171 x 218 mm (6¾″ x 8%₁₆″)
No watermark
RL 12569

Cat. 3 is one of the most spontaneous and unselfconscious drawings of Leonardo's early years. It is drawn from a model, using two basic positions of the body, from the front with the bust turned to the left, and from behind looking over the left shoulder. On these foundations Leonardo investigated eighteen positions for the head, concentrating on the torsion of the neck and the fall of light on the skin. In one sketch only – at the centre of the sheet, around the early collector's number 49 – did he show the position of an arm, bent at the elbow to rest the back of the hand against the waist.

The drawing is very close in both style and technique to the studies of a baby, cat. 4, where there is no dominant pose: in the three sketches where we can discern the infant's action, the iconography changes. In the study at the upper left, the child is suckling; to the lower right of this, he places a hand in his mouth (perhaps to eat a Eucharistic grape, perhaps to suck his thumb); and in the smaller sketch to the lower left, he twists, apparently to give a blessing. The subsidiary drawings of the infant's limbs were probably drawn simply to study the folds of fat – the Christ Child in Florentine painting of the second half of the fifteenth century often reached grotesque degrees of plumpness.

Both sheets are presumably related to Leonardo's sequence of *Madonna and Child* compositions of the latter half of the 1470s, but it is futile to try to identify drawings such as cats. 3 and 4 as studies for particular paintings unless the correspondences of motif are strikingly close.

cat. 3

cat. 4

5
Heads in profile

ca. 1478
Pen and ink
402 x 290 mm (15¹³⁄₁₆″ x 11⁷⁄₁₆″)
Watermark: ladder, close to Briquet 5911
RL 12276v

The profile held a peculiar fascination for Leonardo. In sheets from all periods of his career, sketches of two standard types in profile are found with almost tedious frequency, a gnarled old man (termed the nutcracker by Kenneth Clark) and an angelic youth (formerly and untenably identified with Leonardo's studio assistant Salaì; but see cat. 60). Both types seem to have been appropriated by Leonardo when he was working with Verrocchio – the youth bears a strong resemblance to the bronze *David* (itself occasionally claimed, for no special reason, as a portrait of the young Leonardo), and the nutcracker profile occurs, usually as a warrior, in several products of Verrocchio's workshop, including marble reliefs, the Colleoni equestrian monument, and Leonardo's own highly finished metalpoint drawing in the British Museum. These two figures would spring readily to Leonardo's pen in an idle moment; being left-handed, his profiles usually face to the right, for a draftsman naturally constructs a profile with his hand 'inside' the face.

Leonardo was not accustomed to drawing female heads – other than in specific compositional contexts, the female form is an uncommon motif in Leonardo's sketches. Although the profile of the woman drawn three times here is little different from that of the idealized youth above, the typically Florentine costume of the half-length study and the relaxed posture of the sketch at centre right would suggest that she was drawn from the life. Like all artists of his day, Leonardo doubtless used friends, assistants and servants as impromptu models, and the same sitter

Fig. 2   Leonardo da Vinci, *A woman in profile*
Metalpoint on uncoloured prepared paper, 318 x 199 mm (12½″ x 7¹³⁄₁₆″). RL 12505

seems to have been portrayed more carefully in a large metalpoint drawing also at Windsor (fig. 2). In that drawing Leonardo abandoned his standard youthful profile and drew only what was before him: we can see the contrast between the mannered products of his imagination and the acute objectivity of which he was

capable when drawing directly from nature.

A profile drawn very similarly to that at the centre left appears on a sheet in the Uffizi (P. 127) inscribed by Leonardo with the date 1478, and the present sheet must have been executed at around the same time.

Fig. 3 Leonardo da Vinci, *The Adoration of the Magi*
Oil on panel, 246 x 243 cm (97″ x 96″). Florence, Gallerie degli Uffizi

The Adoration
of the Magi

6
Studies of horses

ca. 1479
Charcoal underdrawing, pen and ink
107 x 183 mm (4³⁄₁₆″ x 7³⁄₁₆″)
Watermark: Calvary (cut), not in Briquet
RL 12324

7
Studies of horses

ca. 1479
Metalpoint and pen and ink on orange
prepared paper
117 x 194 mm (4⅝″ x 7⅝″)
No watermark
RL 12325

8
Studies of asses and an ox

ca. 1480
Charcoal and pen and ink
164 x 177 mm (6⁷⁄₁₆″ x 7″)
No watermark
RL 12362

9
Studies of a horse

ca. 1481
Metalpoint on off-white prepared paper
114 x 196 mm (4½″ x ¾″)
No watermark
RL 12315

The earliest large group of drawings by Leonardo to survive is on the theme of the Adoration. Drawings in Bayonne and Venice (P. 39–40B) show the Madonna kneeling over the Christ Child, surrounded by bystanders, including another infant, presumably the Baptist, whom Christ blesses in both the Venice sheets. The most complete compositional study is in the Louvre (fig. 4), where the Child is held in the Madonna's lap and examines a gift proffered by a kneeling old man; the subject is thus the *Adoration of the Magi*. There are related sheets of figure studies in Hamburg, Cologne, the British Museum and the Ecole des Beaux-Arts (P. 41, 43–44, 46–49), and a number of studies of horses, oxen and asses at Windsor and elsewhere (P. 54–59, 63B–65, including cats. 6–9).

Many of these drawings can be connected directly with Leonardo's first masterpiece, the unfinished *Adoration of the Magi* (fig. 3), now in the Uffizi along with the most elaborate of his *Adoration* drawings, a perspective study for the background of the panel populated by men,

cat. 6

horses and a prominent camel (P. 53). The painting is universally accepted to be that commissioned from Leonardo in March 1481 (though it has been contended that this date should be interpreted as March 1480) by the monks of San Donato a Scopeto outside Florence, and abandoned when Leonardo left the city later in 1481. The painting is far more grand in scale and concept than the Bayonne and Venice drawings, which seem to show instead the *Adoration of the Shepherds*; from their homely types to the mysterious, ecstatic figures of the panel and the studies most closely related to it there is a stylistic and conceptual development too profound to have occurred in the six months or so between the signing of the contract and Leonardo's abandonment of the project.

For this reason it has been proposed that before he received the San Donato commission Leonardo had worked on a separate painting of the *Adoration of the Shepherds*, for which the earlier drawings of the group are studies. While accepting that there is no more evidence against this hypothesis than there is for it, it may not be necessary to posit two separate projects. Artists often began work on the composition of a painting before the contract was signed, for such contracts often included drawings of an agreed design, and we may reasonably extend Leonardo's interest in the San Donato project to some time before 1481.

The San Donato commission stemmed from the endowment of a saddle-maker in 1479, which provided for a painting for the high altar of the monastery and a

cat. 7

cat. 8

dowry for his granddaughter. Leonardo's father was the notary for San Donato and he presumably played a significant role in obtaining the commission for his son; it may be that Leonardo began thinking about the altarpiece as early as 1479, as soon as the commission became a possibility, and that his initial ideas for a conventional Florentine *Adoration of the Shepherds* had evolved into an elaborate

Adoration of the Magi, accommodating many more figures, by the time the contract was signed.

It is clear that much of the underpainting was improvised directly on the panel, and Leonardo may not have been fully aware of the hopelessly ambitious nature of the fantasy he was creating. The deep and sustained thought that lay behind his evolution of the composition

was a turning point in his career. His previous paintings were little different in concept from those of his contemporaries, but this was something startlingly original, and must have given him a powerful awareness of the potential of his art and – more ominously – of the limitations of the hand in realising the products of the mind. The contract gave Leonardo between twenty-four and thirty months

to complete the painting; instead he fled Florence, and the monks waited fifteen years for Leonardo's return before commissioning a substitute from Filippino Lippi.

Of the four drawings here, cat. 9 is much the closest in spirit to the final painting, although this particular motif does not appear there. A highly strung stallion rears in a lunar light, not engaging with the spectator but seen from afar, like the phantoms inhabiting the perspective of the Uffizi drawing.

In complete contrast is cat. 8, a prosaic drawing of an ox and an ass. These animals were drawn in with the brush in a similar pose in the right background of the panel, but stylistically they belong to the moment of the Louvre drawing (fig. 3) and are thus datable to around 1480.

To their left, the charcoal sketch, almost rubbed away, of a man reaching down from the back of an ass is presumably connected with the procession visible in the background of the Louvre composition.

Cats. 6 and 7 are rather harder to place. If judged by the poor rendering of the horse's anatomy, they must be earlier than cats. 8 and 9, and may be among Leonardo's first attempts to come to terms with the animal's form, which he had mastered by the time he drew cat. 9. The bony rear quarters of the horse on the right of cat. 6 are repeated in RL 12308, a drawing on a distinctive purple ground of exactly the same colour as the early Hamburg drawing for the *Adoration* (P. 41); it would thus be reasonable to assume that they are all of the same date, *ca.* 1479.

1481–1500
Mainly Milan

Leonardo is last documented in Florence on 28 September 1481, and nothing is known of his whereabouts for the next year and a half. It is not impossible that he cut his losses on the *Adoration of the Magi* and travelled to Rome, hoping to find some employment on what was then the most extensive artistic project in Italy – the frescos in the Sistine Chapel, the contracts for most of which were awarded to Ghirlandaio, Botticelli, Perugino and Cosimo Rosselli on 27 October 1481. The unfinished and undocumented *St Jerome* (Vatican Galleries) must have been executed at around this time; it has an (admittedly late) Roman provenance, and was conceivably worked on by Leonardo while he was in the city for a few months in 1481–82. But this is stacking hypothesis on hypothesis.

Whatever Leonardo's movements were for those eighteen months, he was in Milan by 25 April 1483, when he and the half-brothers Ambrogio and Evangelista de Predis received the contract for an altarpiece for the church of San Francesco Grande. Leonardo's reasons for travelling to Milan are not recorded in contemporary documents; one of his earliest biographers, the so called Anonimo Gaddiano (*ca.* 1540), stated that, at the age of thirty (that is, during the twelve months before the San Francesco Grande commission), Leonardo was sent to Milan at the command of Lorenzo de' Medici to present a lyre to the Duke, and there is no good reason to doubt a statement as precise as this.

The San Francesco Grande commission had the most complicated history of any in Leonardo's tortuous career, and the recent discovery of additional documents has not clarified matters. What was finally installed in the church in 1508 was the panel of the *Virgin of the Rocks* now in the National Gallery, London, flanked by side-panels of musical angels; the crystalline appearance of this painting, comparable to the still life on the table in the *Last Supper*, would suggest that most of it was executed in the 1490s, probably with some workshop assistance, although it was perhaps not carried to completion until the following decade. The Louvre version of the same composition, which for whatever reason was diverted from its original destination, is wholly autograph and can on grounds of style be dated to no more than a few years after the signing of the initial contract.

In 1485, Leonardo probably received a commission for a *Nativity* for the King of Hungary, as a diplomatic gift from the

Detail of cat. 24

Sforza court. Two portraits by Leonardo can be dated to the 1480s, the *Musician* in Milan and the *Lady with an ermine* in Cracow, the latter almost certainly a portrait of Cecilia Gallerani, a prominent figure at the Sforza court. The period also marks Leonardo's expansion into technical matters. His first surviving notebook, Paris MS. B, was compiled mostly in the mid- to late 1480s, and contains many drawings of architecture and of military devices; during 1487 he received several payments for his work on a model for the cupola of Milan Cathedral, and in 1490 he visited the Duomo of Pavia as an architectural consultant with Francesco di Giorgio. But Leonardo's real achievements as an architect at this time are very difficult to pin down, and it seems that he rarely went beyond suggesting designs in a general sense, leaving the practical details and direction of any work to a professional architect (see Schofield 1991).

It is likely that the well known draft of a letter (C.A. f. 391r–a) to Ludovico Sforza, effective ruler of Milan, setting out Leonardo's talents in an attempt to obtain employment at the court was not written whilst the artist was still in Florence (as pointed out by Carlo Pedretti and expanded by Schofield). There is thus no basis for dating this letter as early as 1482, and indeed no hard evidence that Leonardo was in the employ of Ludovico before July 1489, when the Florentine ambassador in Milan informed Lorenzo de' Medici that Ludovico was not confident that Leonardo knew how to complete the work on the equestrian monument to Francesco Sforza, Ludovico's father (see cats. 23–27). In April 1490 Leonardo noted "I recommenced the horse", and much of the next three years must have been taken up with his work on this sculpture. By December 1493 the model was ready for casting; but the bronze was requisitioned for military use,

and probably soon after this date Leonardo began to plan his great mural of the *Last Supper*, which he was working on until at least 1497 (cats. 29–31).

During the 1480s Leonardo began his significant scientific studies. He started to assemble a small library, and from the later 1480s he taught himself some Latin, in which nearly all treatises were written, but he was never at ease with the language. From a combination of received wisdom and personal experience Leonardo began to record observations on light and colour, perspective and optics, dynamics and statics, primarily in terms of the mathematical laws and proportional harmonies that he perceived behind the apparent complexity of Creation. In parallel with these studies of the physical sciences, most of which were directed towards a projected treatise on painting, he also laid out his thoughts for a treatise on the human body, covering the organic processes that constitute life as well as anatomy and physiology. The first certain date for Leonardo's work on anatomy is April 1489, when he commenced the so called Anatomical MS. B, including the exquisite series of skull drawings (cats. 20–21), but there are a number of less accomplished studies, including several of animals, that must have been executed a couple of years earlier.

Leonardo's artistic activities after the completion of the *Last Supper* centred on the decoration of the Sala delle Asse in the Castello Sforzesco; the portrait known as the *Belle Ferronière* (Louvre) probably dates from the same period. Leonardo continued in Ludovico's favour – in October 1498 the Duke gave him a vineyard – but within a year his patron had fallen from power. The French under Louis XII (who had an ancestral claim to the Duchy of Milan) invaded Lombardy in August 1499; Ludovico fled Milan, the

commander of the Castello was bribed to capitulate, and Louis entered the city in triumph on 6 October 1499.

Two months later Leonardo arranged for 600 gold florins to be transferred to his account at Santa Maria Nuova in Florence, and left Milan for Venice in the company of the mathematician Luca Pacioli. His reason for leaving was not loyalty to Ludovico (a quality that troubled Leonardo little); Venice was allied with France, and Leonardo was possibly sent to the city by the French in an official capacity, with Pacioli, who knew the area, as his guide. By March 1500 he had reached Venice, having passed through Mantua where he drew a portrait of the Marchesa and great collector Isabella d'Este (Louvre, P. 172). In Venice Leonardo advised the Senate on the defence of the city's mainland territory against the advancing Turks, but he stayed in the city only a few weeks, and his impact on Venetian art is tantalizingly hard to define. There is some evidence that Leonardo also visited Rome (a week's ride from Venice) in March, but by the end of the month he was back in Florence, now a republic, to begin the busiest decade of his career.

Early mechanical studies

10
Designs for war chariots and weapons

ca. 1483–85
Stylus underdrawing, pen and ink with wash
200 x 278 mm (7⅞″ x 10¹⁵⁄₁₆″)
No watermark
RL 12653

11
Designs for mortars and gun barrels

ca. 1483–85
Pen and ink
282 x 205 mm (11⅛″ x 8¹⁄₁₆″)
No watermark
RL 12652

12
Designs for a boat, a canoe, etc

ca. 1485–87
Charcoal underdrawing, pen and ink
208 x 288 mm (8³⁄₁₆″ x 11⁵⁄₁₆″)
No watermark
RL 12649

Before the development of moderately reliable mixes of gunpowder in the sixteenth century, military combat was essentially a manual affair, and treatises abounded with often far-fetched devices intended to give an army a decisive advantage. Although the materials available, and the accuracy and speed of manufacture in the pre-industrial age, were such as to make all but the most basic of machines impractical for warfare, this was no impediment to the imagination, and Leonardo's previously cited draft letter to Ludovico Sforza is as grand and vague as any contemporary treatise: "I have methods for

cat. 10

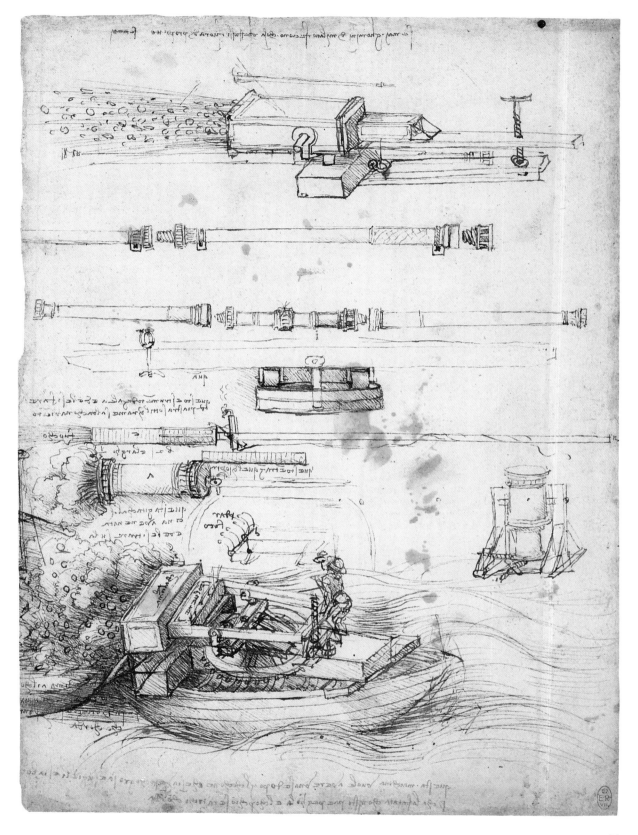

cat. 11

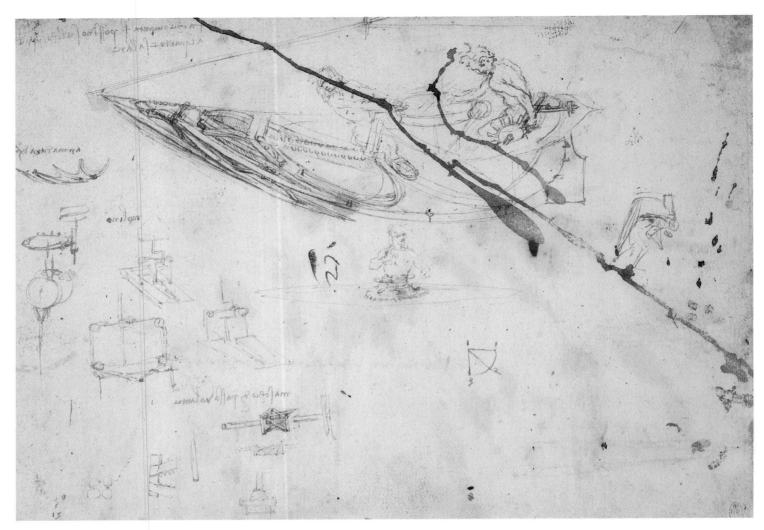

destroying every rock or other fortress ... I have kinds of mortars, most convenient and easy to carry, and with these I can fling small stones almost resembling a storm ... If the fight should be at sea, I have many kinds of machines most efficient for offence and defence, and vessels which will resist the attack of the largest guns and powder ... I will make covered chariots, safe and unattackable ... In case of need I will make big guns, mortars and light ordnance of fine and useful type ... I would contrive catapults, mangonels, trabuchs and other machines of marvellous efficacy and not in common use ..." (C.A. f. 391r–a).

The chariots drawn in cat. 10 are apparently not inventions by Leonardo, and depict weapons described in the writings of ancient authors. As the chariots are pulled along, the wheels cause the central axis to turn, throwing outwards the cannonballs and spiked clubs. In other sheets Leonardo developed this idea with revolving scythes, to be ridden into the ranks of the opposing infantry to gruesome effect.

Cat. 11 shows a number of designs for gun barrels and mortars, the most elaborate of which is mounted with a turntable on a rather unstable boat. Leonardo adopted a combination of screws and a

toothed wheel which could have aimed the mortars very precisely, though their short-barrel design would have obtained only a broad scatter. Indeed the words *polvere* (powder) and *chalcina* (lime) written on the boxes below, and *fuocho* (fire) in the spray from the circular barrel at centre, show that the mortars were intended to discharge 'Greek fire', a burning mixture of powders and resins so called from its use by the Byzantine Greeks during the medieval sieges of Constantinople.

The long gun barrels of cat. 11, by contrast, were conceived as fine pieces of engineering. The turntable at the centre of the sheet is a cradle for mounting the gun above, with two opposed barrels so that one could be loaded while the other was being fired. Below this is a device for a lever-mounted tinder that could be operated by string from the end of a long pole – the unpredictable nature of gunpowder mixes in the fifteenth century frequently caused gun barrels to explode rather than discharge their missiles.

Cat. 12 is less obviously military in nature. The main drawing seems to show a mechanically operated boat that could be folded up and carried on the back, as seen in the rapid sketch at centre right. It may be possible to relate the principle of this collapsible boat to another passage in Leonardo's letter to Duke Ludovico where he claims that "I have a sort of extremely light and strong bridge, adapted to be most easily carried". The paler sketch at the centre of the sheet has been interpreted as a diving bell, but the pen-lines to either side of the figure suggest that it is a design for a canoe, with a seal around the waist of the occupant. The drawings of wheels, joints and so on to the lower left of the sheet are too crudely drawn to be interpreted.

13

Pictographs, and the ground plan of a palazzo

ca. 1487–90
Stylus underdrawing, pen and ink
300 x 253 mm (11¹³⁄₁₆″ x 9¹⁵⁄₁₆″)
No watermark
RL 12692v

Rebuses, pictorial puns and other cryptograms were beloved of the fifteenth century, particularly in courtly circles. Here Leonardo tries his hand at pictographs – picture writing formed from a combination of some objects which stand for themselves, other objects and symbols that are homophonous with grammatical structures, and a few linking letters. A good example is the sequence in a darker ink at the centre of the upper half of the sheet, which shows, from right to left with Leonardo's inscriptions below: a pear tree (*pero*); a saddle (*sella*); a woman with a sail, the figure of Fortune (*fortuna*); a musical score with two notes (*mi fa*); a fern (*felice*); the letters *Ta*; a face (*viso*); and, after a gap, a black yarnwinder (*aspo nero*). This gives the fragmentary phrase *Però se la Fortuna mi fa felice tal viso ... asponerò ...*, "Should Fortune make this countenance happy ... I will display ...", of a wistfulness commonly found in Leonardo's writings.

The groups of pictographs here do not form any sequence, nor do they have a common theme. Leonardo was simply exercising his mind, exploring the limitations of the genre by attempting to make coherent phrases using as few letters as possible. Occasionally he would try to make a phrase using pictographs mainly of one type, such as the fish-hook followed by a musical score at upper left, which makes *l'amo re mi fa sol la [za] re*, or *l'amore mi fa sollazzare*, loosely "love gives me pleasure".

Leonardo's obsessive streak is evident in the relentless filling of the sheet, in which he utilizes the spaces in a carefully constructed architectural plan that he had drawn earlier. This and another drawing of the same plan on an identical scale in the Codex Atlanticus (f. 80r–a) are the only fully measured ground plans of a building by Leonardo to survive (but see cats. 49–50 and 56–57). It has been suggested that they relate to a remodelling of the Corte Vecchia, on the site of the present Palazzo Reale in Milan, where Leonardo had his apartments and workshop.

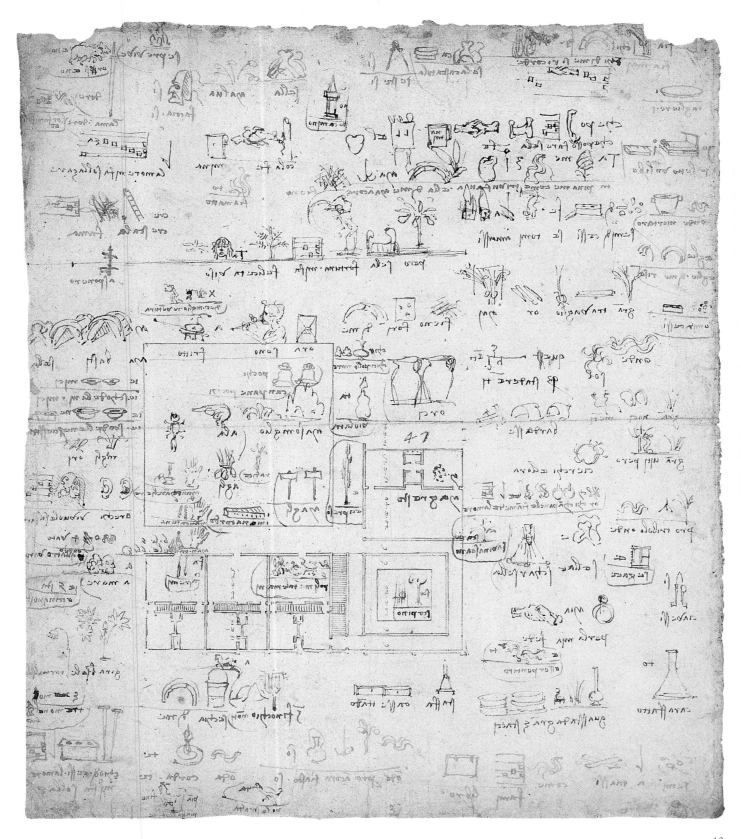

14

Two grotesque profiles

ca. 1487–90
Pen and ink with some wash
163 x 143 mm (6⁷⁄₁₆″ x 5⅝″)
Watermark: the letter P, not in Briquet
RL 12490

Leonardo's use of hatching with the pen
was at its most emphatic in the latter half
of the 1480s, and here is perfectly suited
to a rather fierce profile with beetling
brows and jutting chin. The less clearly
articulated facing profile is that of an old
woman, with her hair drawn back and
her left arm tucked under her trussed
bosom. Leonardo occasionally placed his
creatures in facing profile to effect a contrast, but the difference in scale between
these two grotesques suggests that they
were not conceived as a pair, and that
their apparent contact – the right hand of
the woman held to the chin of the man –
is accidental.

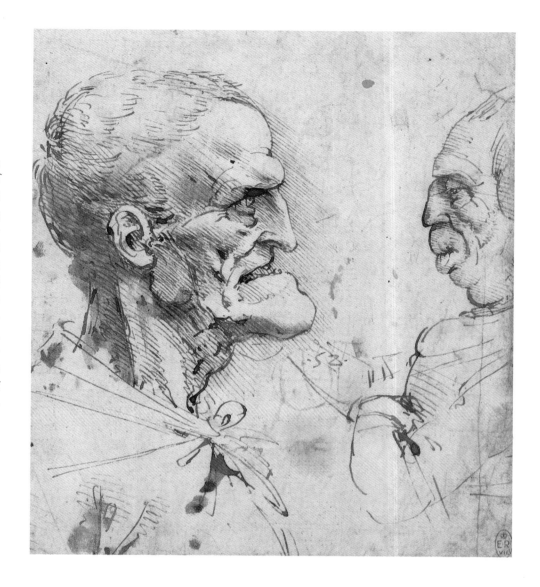

15

An ill-matched couple

ca. 1490
Some charcoal underdrawing, pen and ink
262 x 123 mm (10⅝″ x 4¹³⁄₁₆″), the top left
corner cut
No watermark
RL 12449

The theme of the ill-matched couple
appeared in European art in the later
fifteenth century and attained great popu-
larity in the North during the next century, although it can be traced in litera-
ture back to antiquity. Its most common
form involved a lecherous old man being
duped by a young woman, often shown
filching his purse while his hands are
otherwise occupied. As such the image
was a satire on both Lust and Avarice, the
two most commonly debated of the seven
Deadly Sins.

Leonardo's treatment is unusual, combining a young man and old woman, and
concentrating on the psychological rather
than the material aspects of the theme.
Neither Lust nor Avarice is shown explicitly: the man slips a ring on the finger
of the woman while casting her an evil
sidelong glance, and we have to construct
the narrative ourselves. Further, Leonardo
introduces a third vice, Vanity, in the figure of the old woman, whose ostentatious
clothing contrasts ridiculously with her
haggard profile.

The old woman was one of Leonardo's
most enduring creations. She recurs in a
number of other drawings by or after
Leonardo, most notably a bust-length
'portrait' in red chalk which must be a
copy after a lost original (fig. 5). This
copy was etched by Hollar as the *Queen of
Tunis* in the seventeenth century and by
Pastorini in the nineteenth, while the
original or some other copy was known
to Quentin Massys, who painted a variant
of which there is a copy in the National
Gallery, London. Finally, one of these

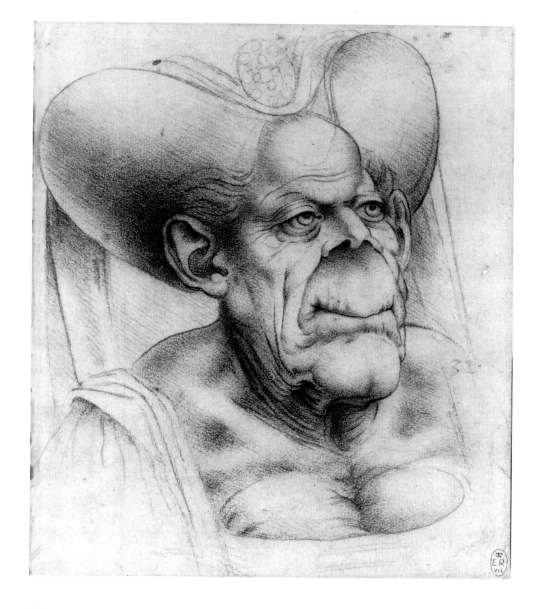

Fig. 5
Attributed to Francesco Melzi, after Leonardo, *A hideous old woman*
Red chalk, 172 x 143 mm (6¾″ x 5⅝″). RL 12492

versions was known to John Tenniel, who used it as the basis for the Ugly Duchess in his illustrations to *Alice's Adventures in Wonderland* (published 1865).

16

A study of the fall of light on a face

ca. 1487–90
Charcoal underdrawing, pen and ink
203 x 143 mm (8″ x 5⅝″)
Watermark: six-petalled flower (cut), close to Briquet 6541
RL 12604

One of the many projects that occupied Leonardo throughout his life and which was never brought to completion was the preparation of a treatise on painting. Theories and observations, particularly on optics, are scattered throughout Leonardo's drawings and notebooks, and his pupil and heir Francesco Melzi attempted to put these thoughts into some kind of order in a manuscript known as the Codex Urbinas (Vatican, Biblioteca Apostolica), a compendium transcribed from Leonardo's notebooks. The two small circles along the right edge of cat. 16 were Melzi's sign to himself that he had copied those two paragraphs, and therefore the sheet must have formed part of a notebook during the sixteenth century. A fragment of an identical watermark is found on RL 12632, one of a number of sheets of *ca.* 1487–90 in which Leonardo reused paper from an administration register of Milan Cathedral.

Leonardo considered the scientifically accurate rendering of light and shade to be central to the art of painting: "Shadows have their boundaries at certain determinable points. He who is ignorant of these will produce work without relief; and relief is the soul and summit of painting" (*Trattato*, § 121). Around 1490, he drew in MS. C a great

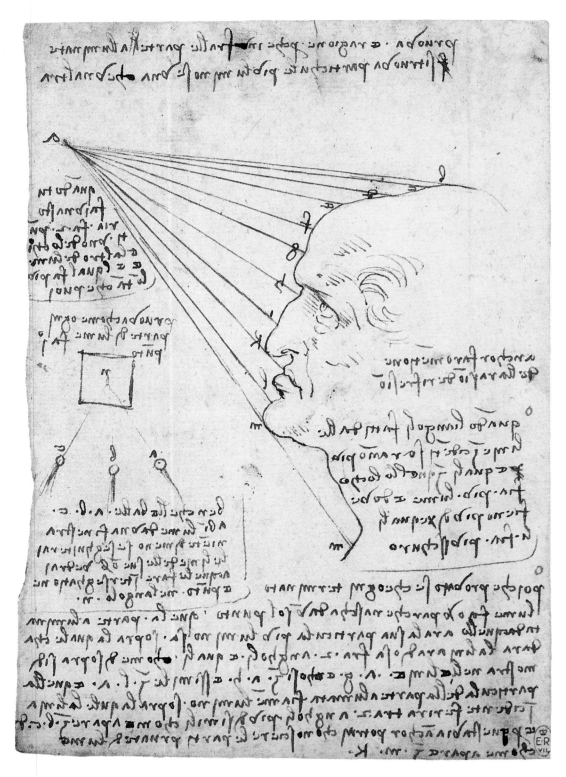

cat. 16

series of diagrams of light falling on the surfaces of spheres and cylinders; the present sheet dates from a couple of years earlier, while his mind was still focussed on applications of immediate use to the artist, and he wrote didactically, addressing the reader in the second person. The drawing and notes consider the gradations of illumination of an object from a single light source, whether point or extended:

Proof and reason why among the illuminated parts certain portions are more illuminated than others.

Although the balls a b c [centre left] *are illuminated from a window, nevertheless, if you follow the lines of their shadows you will see that they intersect at a point* n.

Since it is proved that every definite light has, or appears to have, its origins in a single point, that part [of an object] *illuminated by it will have that portion more illuminated on to which the radiant line falls perpendicularly, as is shown above in the lines* ag, *and also* ah, *and similarly* la; *and that portion of the illuminated part will be less illuminated where the incident line strikes it more glancingly, as is seen at* b c d; *and by this means you may also know the parts deprived of light, as is seen at* m *and* k.

17

Studies of the nervous system

ca. 1487
Metalpoint and pen and ink on pale-blue prepared paper
298 x 225 mm (11¾″ x 8⅞″)
No watermark visible
RL 12613v

Cat. 17 is one of a number of sheets from the 1480s in which the original metalpoint drawing has faded to invisibility. All that remain to the naked eye are the pen-and-ink outlines with which Leonardo strengthened his metalpoint, suggesting that illegibility was a very early problem.

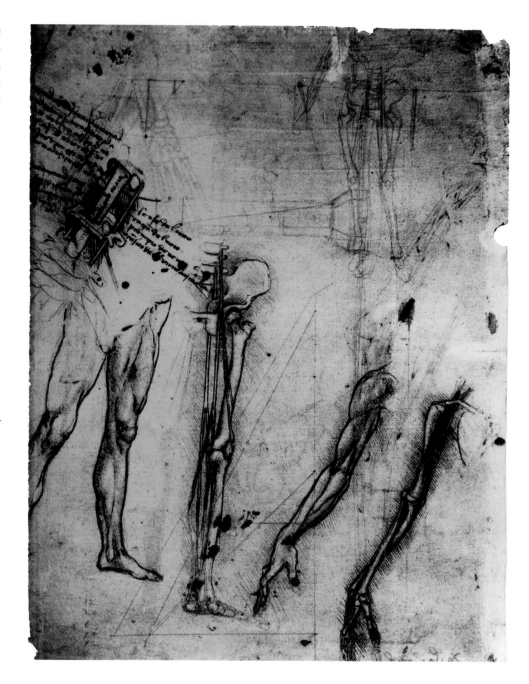

Cat. 17 in ultraviolet light

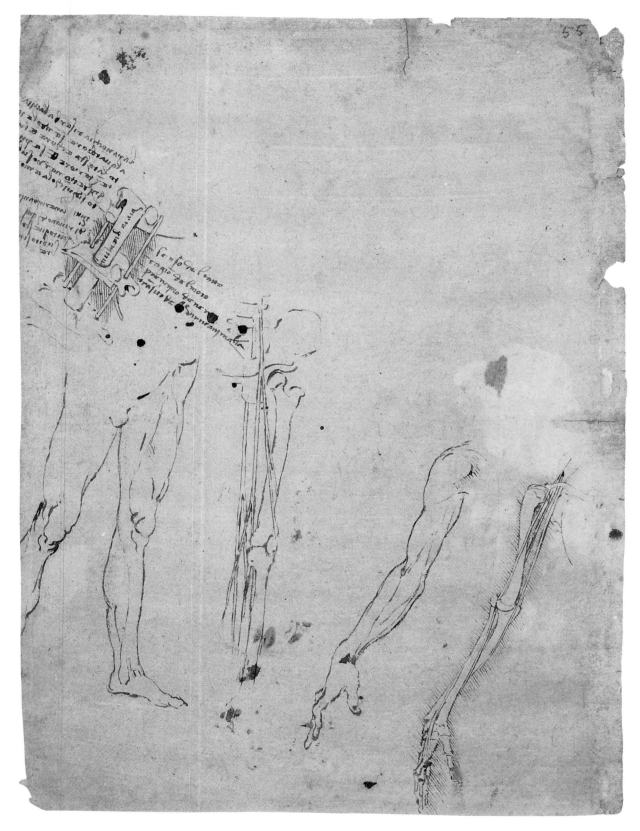

cat. 17

The chemical behaviour of metalpoint over time is poorly understood, and there is no obvious reason why drawings on some sheets should have faded while others remain as strong as the day they were drawn. Ultraviolet light reveals (albeit weakly) the original extent of the drawings, including a number of geometrical constructions and a surprisingly accurate study of the lower half of the skeleton with the nerves sketched in.

The four lower pen-drawings show the legs alongside a corresponding diagram of the bones with the femoral and sciatic nerves, and the right arm with its bones and the ulnar, radial and median nerves. The shape of the humerus suggests that Leonardo had actually dissected a monkey and adjusted its proportions to correspond to the arm of a man.

Leonardo's early plans for a treatise on human anatomy were far more ambitious in their scope than such modern treatises. The earliest surviving list of topics to be covered (RL 19037v, *ca.* 1489) mentions morphology as only a small portion of the work: "... describe how [men and women] are composed of veins, nerves, muscles and bones. This you will do at the end of the book." The bulk of the intended material was to be concerned with the phenomena of life: conception and birth, the growth of the child, the emotions and the senses. The drawing at upper left on cat. 17 is a schematic rendering of the cervical vertebrae, with the spinal cord at the centre; along this Leonardo has written *generative power*, echoing the Aristotelian belief that conception required both a material and a spiritual contribution from both parents, and that the latter 'animal spirit' flowed from the brain down the spinal cord to the reproductive organs.

The accompanying note recounts one of Leonardo's few experiments with vivisection: *The frog retains life for some hours when deprived of its head and heart and all its bowels. And if you puncture the said nerve* [spinal medulla] *it immediately twitches and dies. All nerves of animals derive from here. When this is pricked the animal dies at once.*

Elements from both the recto and the verso of cat. 17, and probably from other sheets of the late 1480s, were copied schematically in reverse by Albrecht Dürer in his Dresden Sketchbook of around 1517. It is highly unlikely that Dürer had access to the originals, and the reversal of the copies and their outline nature suggests that he was working from long vanished tracings – or even prints – after Leonardo's drawings.

18

The proportions of the head

ca. 1488–89
Metalpoint and pen and ink on blue prepared paper
213 x 153 mm (8⅜″ x 6″)
No watermark
RL 12601

Most theorists of art in the Renaissance concerned themselves at some stage with human proportion, following the traditional belief in the existence of fixed and harmonious ratios within and between the components of the Universe – the search for a canon of ideal beauty was, in principle, no abstract exercise. As part of his researches towards his projected treatises on painting and anatomy, Leonardo was deeply interested in proportion in the years around 1490, producing at this time his iconic image of the Vitruvian man (Accademia, Venice), whose outstretched limbs fit into the perfect shapes of square and circle.

In style and technique the present sheet is a little earlier than the majority of the proportion drawings, and closer to the first phase of studies for the Sforza monument (cat. 23), around 1488–89. There is little of obvious practical use to the artist in the accompanying note: *There is as much from* a *to* b*, the origin of the hairs in front to the line of the top of the head, as there is from* c *to* d*, that is, from the end of the nose below, to the junction of the lips at the front of the mouth. It is as much from the teardurt of the eye* m *to the top of the head* a*, as it is from* m *to below the chin* s. s c f b *are equal to one another as to distance.*

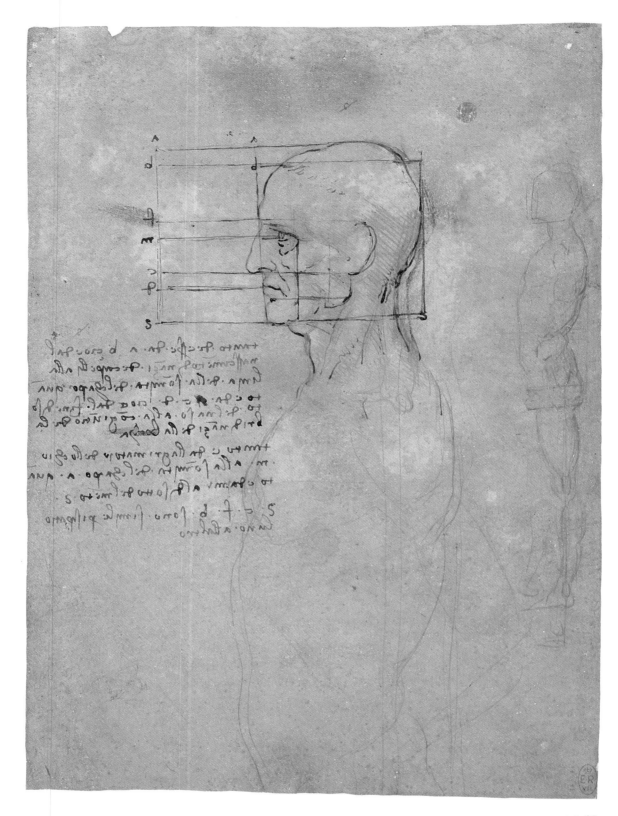

cat. 18

19

A male nude from the back and side

ca. 1490
Metalpoint with white heightening on blue
prepared paper
177 x 140 mm (7″ x 5½″)
No watermark
RL 12637

This beautiful sheet of studies from the life shows the full range of finish in Leonardo's metalpoint drawings, from the most rapid lines to a dense surface of tightly hatched shading with carefully applied white heightening. Stylistically the drawing is very close to several of the studies towards the Sforza monument (*e.g.* cat. 25), and also shows, between the legs and along the lower line of the buttocks, a couple of the proportional or constructional lines that characterize those sheets. The purpose of the drawing is unknown, but it may have been made in connection with Leonardo's work on proportion around 1490.

20

Studies of a skull

1489
Pen and ink
189 x 139 mm (7⁷⁄₁₆″ x 5½″)
Watermark: the letter A surmounted by a
crown (cut), close to Briquet 7933
RL 19059

21

A skull sectioned

1489
Slight charcoal underdrawing, pen and ink
190 x 137 mm (7½″ x 5⅜″)
Watermark: as cat. 20
RL 19058v

A series of drawings of the human skull is the outstanding achievement of Leonardo's early anatomical work. Cat. 20 carries the inscription *On the 2nd day of April 1489. Book entitled On the Human Figure*, and while this date must refer simply to the start of Leonardo's work on the manuscript, all the skull studies can with some confidence be placed in that year, providing the first firm date for Leonardo's anatomical work.

The two drawings on cat. 20 show both the superficial temporal vein and a portion of the maxillary; in the accompanying note Leonardo traced its infraorbital branch, joining the lacrimal branches of the ophthalmic vessels and descending through the infraorbital foramen, to run along the orbital margin and connect with other branches of the ophthalmic vessels joining the angular and frontal veins.

Cat. 21 is one of Leonardo's most compelling anatomical studies. The skull has been sectioned sagitally, then the right half frontally, and the two halves juxtaposed. This allows one to locate the cavities in relation to the surface features: cover the right half of the drawing to see how much less legible a complete frontal section would have been. The presentation of the material is masterly, and after five hundred years the image is occasionally used today in lectures to medical students.

Leonardo's main concern in cat. 21 is the relative depths of the facial cavities. The note below the main drawing reads: *The cavity of the eye socket, and the cavity in the bone that supports the cheek, and those of the nose and mouth, are of equal depth and terminate in a perpendicular line below the* senso comune. *And each of these cavities is as deep as the third part of a man's face, that is, from the chin to the hair.*

The drawing thus combines Leonardo's interests at this time in both proportion and the location of the mental faculties. Lacking any evidence to the contrary, he followed the medieval tradition that the brain contained three bulbous ventricles, leading back in a straight line behind the eyes. The ventricles housed the *senso comune*, the intellectual and imaginative faculties, and the memory. The *senso comune* was the supposed site upon which all the sensory nerves converged, the interface between the world and the mind; to Leonardo, the self-proclaimed "disciple of experience", the *senso comune* was thus the centre of man's being. It was natural for one who believed in the universality of proportion to locate this at the geometrical centre of the head, and several of the 1489 skull studies (including the recto and verso of cat. 21) detail its position in relation to the features of the skull.

The marginal note on cat. 21 describes the teeth, drawn and numbered above: Leonardo included both sides of the mouth to give four incisors, two canines, four premolars and six molars (with the wisdom teeth erupted) for both upper and lower jaw. The accuracy of this count may seem trivial, but there was much confusion at the time about the number of human teeth, including the perpetuation of Aristotle's claim that women have fewer teeth than men.

Detail of cat. 21

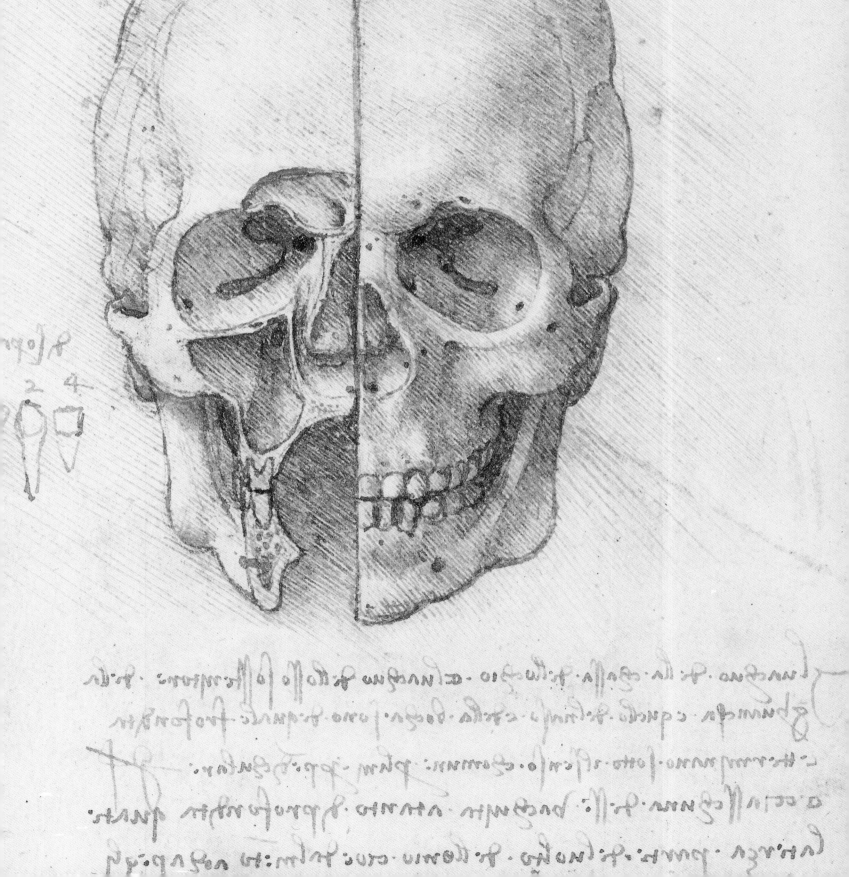

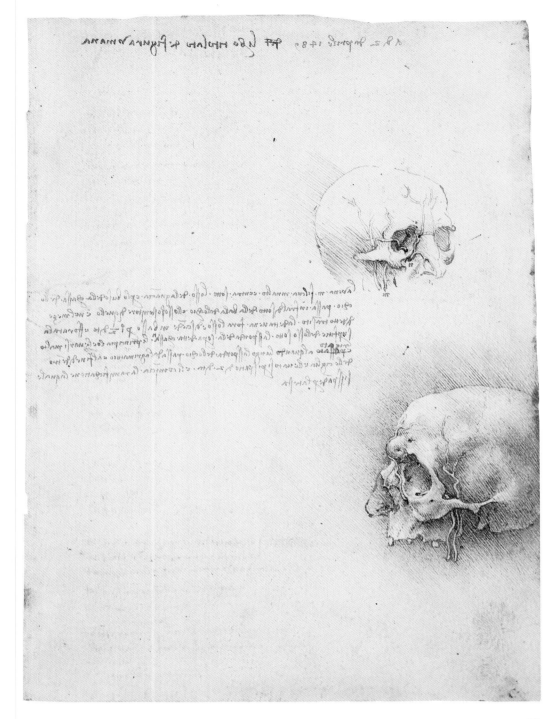

cat. 20

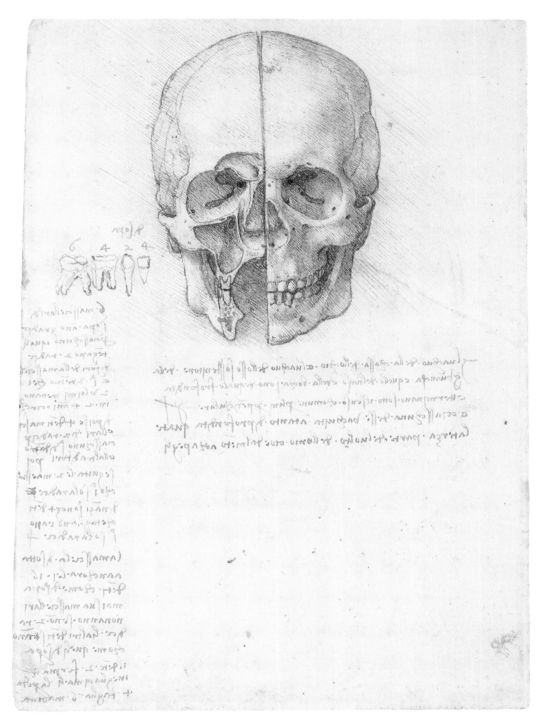

cat. 21

22

A bear's leg dissected

ca. 1490
Metalpoint and pen and ink, with white
heightening, on pale blue-grey prepared paper
162 x 137 mm (6⅜″ x 5⅜″)
No watermark
RL 12372

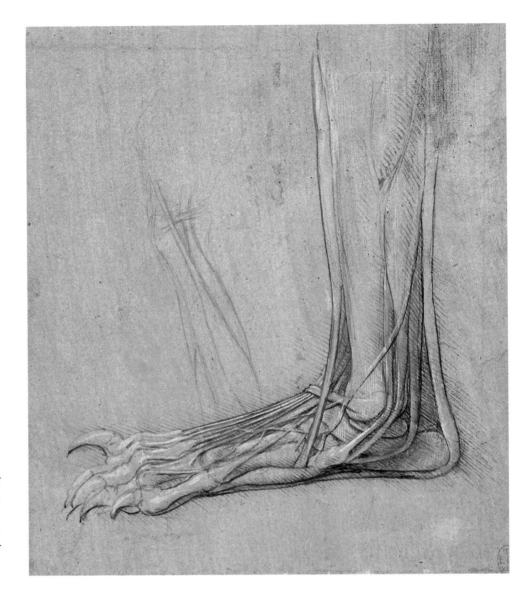

Throughout his career Leonardo was
interested in comparative anatomy. Although he never abandoned the traditional belief that all mammals were fun-
damentally similar in the systems of their
anatomy, the differences lying only in
their proportions, he investigated the variations of detail peculiar to several species.
According to Vasari he even compiled a
treatise on the anatomy of the horse, now
lost, in connection with his work on the
Sforza equestrian monument (see cats.
23–27).

Bears lived wild and were hunted in
Italy in the fifteenth century; they were
also kept in captivity by street entertain-
ers and for baiting. Leonardo would have
had little difficulty obtaining the leg of a
bear for dissection, and five drawings of
the bones, muscles and tendons of a left
hind leg survive at Windsor (cat. 22 and
RL 12373–75). In style and technique
they are close to the second series of
drawings for the Sforza monument (*e.g.*
cat. 25), and thus datable around 1490.

The bear's-foot drawings and the skull
series (cats. 20–21) stand out among Leonardo's early anatomical work in being
wholly objective, and they reinforce the
general impression that he had little, if
any, access to satisfactory human dissection material in his early years (it must be
emphasized that human dissection was
not proscribed by the Church, subject to
certain reasonable regulations). His drawings from this period that purport to
show soft-tissue human anatomy are syn-
theses of tradition, assumed physiology,
surface observation and animal dissection,

and they are accordingly inaccurate. But
when Leonardo restricted himself to
recording only what was before him, as
here, he was capable of great acuity, foreshadowing the spectacular achievements
of twenty years later (cats. 67–71).

The Sforza monument

23

A study for the Sforza monument

ca. 1488–89. Metalpoint on blue prepared paper, 148 x 185 mm (5¹³⁄₁₆″ x 7⁵⁄₁₆″)
No watermark. RL 12358

24

Studies of a horse

ca. 1490. Metalpoint on pale pinkish-buff prepared paper, 200 x 284 mm (7⅞″ x 11³⁄₁₆″)
No watermark. RL 12317

25

A study of a horse from the front

ca. 1490–91. Metalpoint on blue prepared paper, 221 x 110 mm (8¹¹⁄₁₆″ x 4⁵⁄₁₆″)
No watermark. RL 12290

26

The measurements of a horse's foreleg

ca. 1491–92. Charcoal underdrawing, pen and ink, 250 x 187 mm (9¹³⁄₁₆″ x 7⅜″)
Watermark: bull's head, close to Briquet 14431
RL 12294

27

Designs for casting apparatus

ca. 1493. Pen and ink, some notes in red chalk 278 x 191 mm (10¹⁵⁄₁₆″ x 7½″)
Watermark: serpent, close to Briquet 13708
RL 12349

An equestrian monument to Francesco Sforza (died 1466) is first mentioned in a letter of November 1473 from his son Galeazzo Maria Sforza to the commissar of the ducal works, instructing him to find an artist capable of carrying out the sculpture. Apparently nothing was done at this time; Galeazzo Maria was mur-

cat. 23

cat.

dered in 1476, and his brother Ludovico went into exile between 1477 and 1479. On his return to Milan, Ludovico revived the project, and we have our first notice of Leonardo's interest in the monument in his undated draft of a letter to Ludovico, through which he hoped to gain employment at the court: "Moreover, I would undertake the work of the bronze horse, which shall be an immortal glory and eternal honour to the auspicious memory of the Prince your father and of the illustrious house of Sforza" (C.A. f. 391r–a).

Although we do not now think of Leonardo as a sculptor – not one work certainly by him has survived – he was clearly considered more than competent in his time. He had trained in Verrocchio's studio, which was in the 1470s the most active and ambitious bronze-casting workshop in Italy, and must have been closely aware of the early stages of work on the Colleoni equestrian monument, the full-scale model of which was complete and ready for transport in pieces from Florence to Venice in 1481. Antonio Pollaiuolo was also interested in obtaining the commission for the Sforza monument, and prepared *modello*-type drawings for Ludovico, two of which have survived; but Leonardo received the commission, possibly as part of a general contract as artist and engineer to the Sforza court.

We have little idea of the progress of the work during the 1480s. Only two drawings for the monument survive from this stage (cat. 23 and RL 12357), together with an invaluable engraving in the British Museum that records four poses for the horse and rider, one of which almost replicates RL 12357. These cannot be closely dated; notes on the verso of cat. 23, which were presumably made after the sketch on the recto, are probably of around 1489. The horses are of the slightly skittish, bottle-nosed type familiar from the *Adoration* studies (cat. 9), and indeed their poses are less convincing sculpturally than they are pictorially. It is perhaps significant that Leonardo seems not to have made studies of horses from the life in the intervening period, and his conception of the form of the horse was still two-dimensional.

All of these early designs show the horse rearing, its forelegs supported either by a tree-stump or by a cowering soldier, the latter of which was a standard motif of antique art on medals and in relief, but not in the round. The difficulties of casting such a piece would have been considerable, and in the summer of 1489 the Florentine ambassador wrote to Lorenzo de' Medici that Ludovico requested the names of other artists who might be more suited to the project, for he was not fully confident that Leonardo understood how to complete the work.

Lorenzo could not oblige Ludovico, but evidently Leonardo overcame the Duke's doubts, for on 23 April 1490 he recorded, "I recommenced the horse". It seems that at this stage he changed from an ambitious rearing pose to a more sober and conventional pacing horse; a number of tiny sketches from around this time, including the drawing in the lower right corner of cat. 24, show a horse walking in profile in the manner of the now destroyed antique equestrian statue in Pavia known as the *Regisole*. It is known that Leonardo visited Pavia, twenty miles south of Milan, in the summer of 1490, but it is inconceivable that he had not seen the *Regisole* before then.

The Sforza horse was Leonardo's main concern for the next three years. The rather tentative spirit of the earlier studies was remedied by a series of studies of horses from the life, some in casual poses, others surveyed more systematically to record their proportions. Cat. 24 shows the new type of horse that Leonardo was to adopt, with heavier limbs and a more

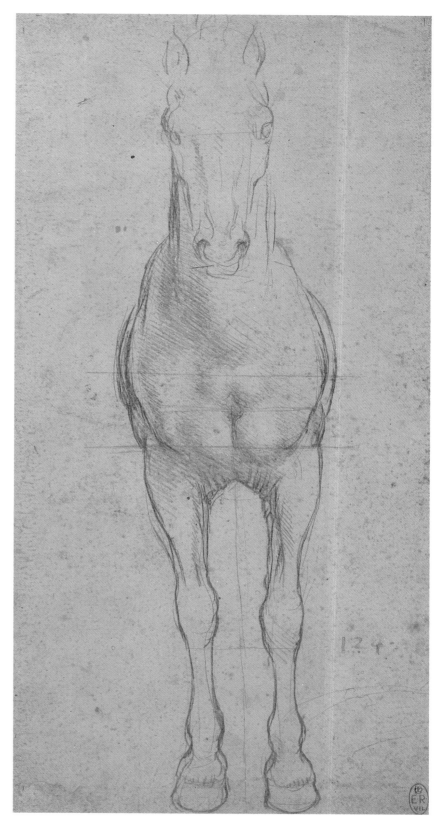

cat. 25

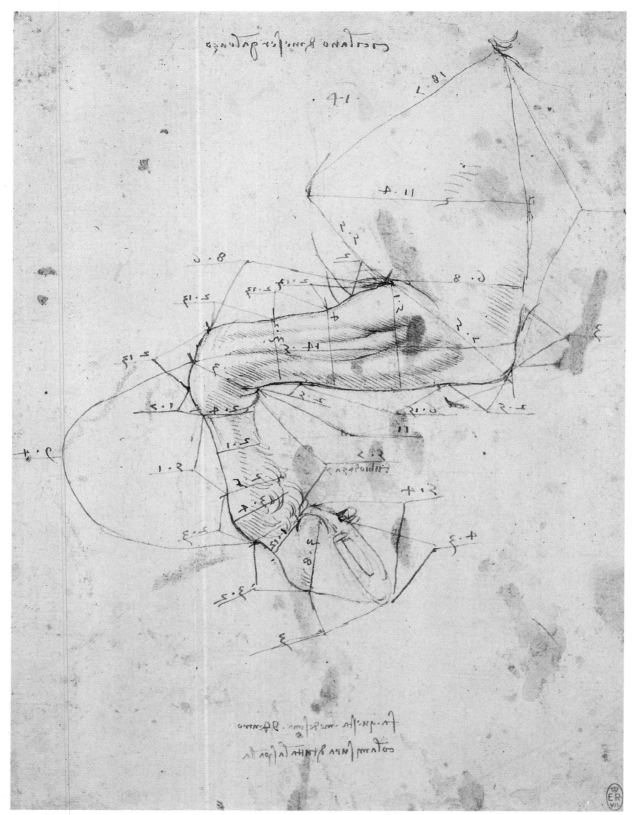

cat. 26

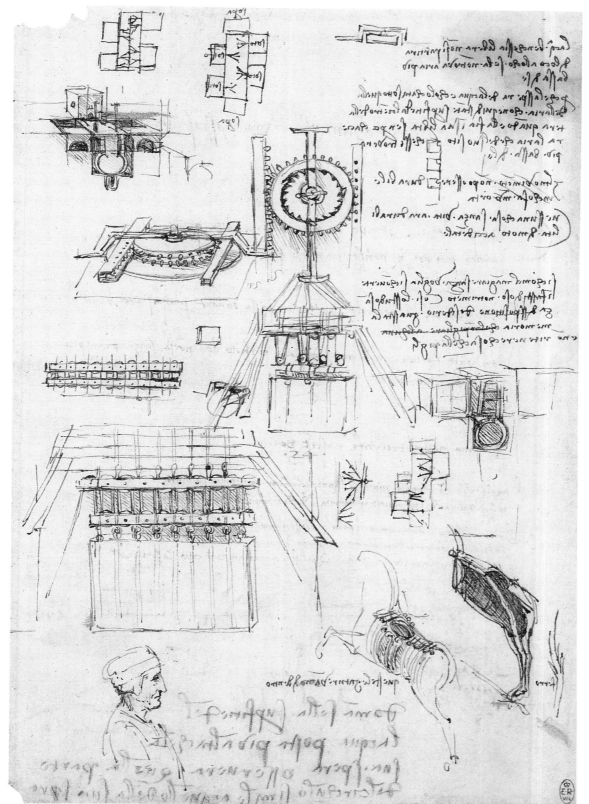

cat. 27

noble head. The confidence with which the bodies are constructed testifies to Leonardo's diligence at studying the anatomy of the horse since the *Adoration of the Magi* ten years earlier (cats. 6–9).

Cat. 25 is one of a series of drawings in metalpoint on blue paper that study the proportions and surface modelling of the horse from the front and side. Here the horse is in the pose of one at the far left of the *Adoration of the Magi* panel (fig. 3), who stares out so disconcertingly at the viewer, and indeed Clark associated the drawing with the *Adoration* panel, preferring the evidence of motif to that of style. But it is stylistically impossible that this drawing could date from around 1480: the drawing is *en suite* with four others (RL 12289, 12319–21) that are unquestionably related to the Sforza project. The lines drawn between the eyes, across the chest and between the legs relate to Leonardo's proportional investigations, which were pursued no further on this sheet, but cat. 26 shows the level of detail to which he took these studies.

The note at the top of cat. 26 records that the horse measured was a Sicilian belonging to Galeazzo da Sanseverino, the Captain-General of the Milanese army. The modelling of the horse's muscles is unnecessary, as the measurements are only of the lengths and thicknesses of the limb; these measurements are apparently in Milanese inches (one-twelfth of a *braccio*, and thus about two modern inches) and sixteenths of an inch. In a note below, Leonardo reminds himself to *make this the same within* [*i.e.* from the other side of the leg], *with the measurement of the whole shoulder.*

The difficulties of the casting must have occupied Leonardo from the start of his work on the project. Compounding the problems associated with any bronze cast was the enormous size of the monument, the horse alone standing

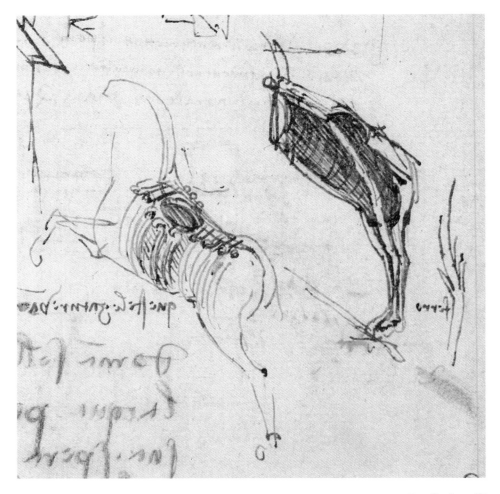

Detail of cat. 27

twenty-four feet high – Verrocchio's Colleoni monument, then the largest bronze cast since antiquity, is thirteen feet high. The sculptor Giuliano da Sangallo was in Milan in October 1492, and Vasari recorded that he advised Leonardo on technical aspects. Cat. 27 shows sketches at upper left and centre right for the casting apparatus, with the horse schematically drawn as a cylinder, upside down with two straight legs pointing upwards. The small branching lines in the geometrical-type drawings are the channels through which the molten metal would run; the largest drawings apparently show the system of pulleys to haul the immense

weight of sculpture and mould out of the ground after casting. The view of the two halves of the sculpture at lower right concentrates on the iron ties holding the entire structure together.

By the autumn of 1493 Leonardo's preparations were approaching completion, and he began to make detailed provisions for casting the huge clay model. On 20 December he recorded, "I have decided to cast the horse without the tail and on its side". But the cast was never made. Military affairs took precedence over artistic ones, and in late 1494 the bronze intended for the horse was sent by Ludovico to his brother-in-law Ercole d'Este in Ferrara to make cannon. Leonardo may have continued to work on the mould (Matteo Bandello recorded that he had seen Leonardo working on the horse and the *Last Supper* concurrently) but without the bronze he could not proceed with the casting. In a draft of a letter of the mid- to late 1490s to the Duke, Leonardo wrote frustratedly, "of the horse I will say nothing, for I know the times ..." (C.A. f. 335v–a).

When Milan was invaded in 1499, the clay model was used for target practice by French archers and destroyed. The deteriorating moulds that had been prepared for the casting were requested from the French by Ercole d'Este in 1501; nothing came of the negotiations, but within ten years, back in Milan, Leonardo was to have a second opportunity to create a bronze equestrian monument.

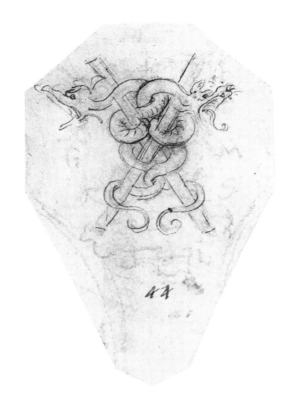

28

An emblem of Galeazzo Maria Sforza (?)

ca. 1495
Black-chalk underdrawing, pen and ink
100 x 66 mm (3¹⁵⁄₁₆″ x 2⁹⁄₁₆″), shaped
No watermark
RL 12282A

This fragment is a design for a heraldic shield, with two snakes twined around a crossed pair of staffs. The viper was the emblem of Milan, adopted both by the Visconti in the earlier part of the century and by the Sforza later, although it was usually represented as a single flattened creature, not, as here, a squirming pair of serpents reaching out of the plane of the device.

It is not certain whose device this was intended to be. Only the letters *G M*, either side of the crossing, are clearly visible; others have claimed to see an *S* below the device, but these strokes are the underdrawing for a ribbon, and a vertical stroke at the upper centre is merely a chance discoloration in the paper. These could be the initials of the young Gian Galeazzo Maria Sforza, Duke of Milan from 1476 to 1494, but in such contexts his initials were usually given as *I* (for Iohannes) *G M. G M* alone would stand instead for Galeazzo Maria Sforza, Gian Galeazzo's father, who died in 1476, before Leonardo arrived in Milan. If the initials do relate to Galeazzo Maria, the shield must have been designed for some commemorative purpose, though from this fragment it is impossible to tell what it might have been, and the device does not appear in any other drawing by Leonardo.

Cat. 28 was cut from a sheet in the Codex Atlanticus (f. 31v–a) by a subsequent owner of Leonardo's papers, probably Pompeo Leoni. On the verso of that sheet is a design for a needle-making machine, which is studied in more detail elsewhere (f. 318v–a) with the note, "Tomorrow morning, 2 January 1496, you will have the strap made and will test it out." The date of *ca.* 1495 that may thus be inferred for cat. 28 is consistent with its technique and style.

The Last Supper

29
The head of Judas

ca. 1495
Red chalk on orange-red prepared paper
180 x 150 mm (7¹⁄₁₆″ x 5⅞″)
No watermark
RL 12547

30
The head of St Philip

ca. 1495
Black chalk
190 x 150 mm (7½″ x 5⅞″)
No watermark
RL 12551

Fig. 6
Leonardo da Vinci, *The Last Supper*
(before restoration)
Oil and tempera on plaster, 460 x 880 cm
(180″ x 350″). Milan, Santa Maria delle Grazie

31
The arm of St Peter

ca. 1495
Black chalk, with white chalk, pen and ink and
white heightening
166 x 155 mm (6⁹⁄₁₆″ x 6⅛″)
No watermark
RL 12546

Cats. 29–31 are preparatory studies for Leonardo's greatest painting, the *Last Supper* (fig. 6) in the refectory of Santa Maria delle Grazie, a monastery church in Milan that was a focus of Sforza patronage in the 1490s. In 1492 work began on a new tribune designed by Bramante, which was later to house the tomb of Ludovico and his wife, Beatrice d'Este, and the painted lunettes above the *Last Supper* testify that it too was commissioned by the Duke.

Our knowledge of the progress of Leonardo's work on the *Last Supper* is very patchy. Two compositional sketches (RL 12542, and a sheet in the Accademia, Venice, P. 162) can be dated to around 1493–94, and Leonardo probably began to paint in the refectory in late 1494 or 1495, after work had halted on the Sforza horse (see cats. 23–27). The only firm date is provided by a letter of 29 June 1497 from Ludovico to his secretary, asking him to press Leonardo to finish the mural so that the artist could begin work on another wall of the refectory. A mention of the painting by Luca Pacioli in his *De divina proportione* of 1498 may suggest that it was completed by that year.

Cat. 29 is a study for the head of Judas in the painting (where a beard was added), and shows better than any other preparatory drawing for the project the essence of Leonardo's intention, to convey psychological states by gesture and expression. But Leonardo was primarily concerned in the drawings with recording physical structure from the life, and it

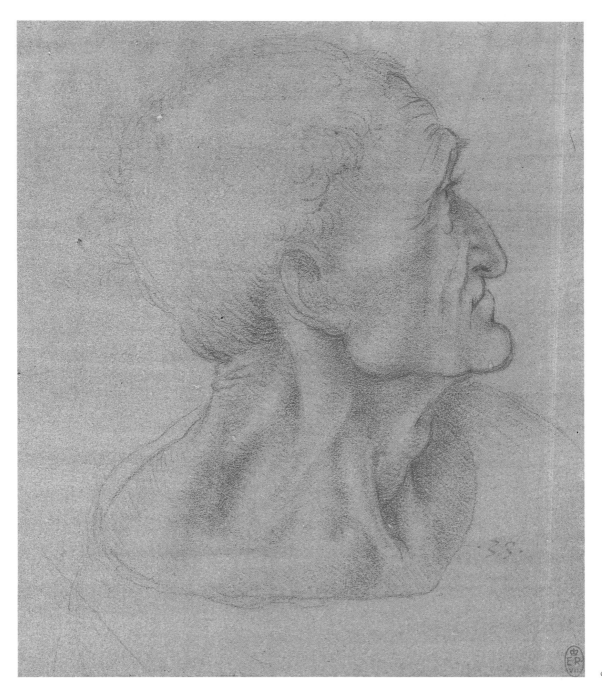

cat. 29

cat. 30

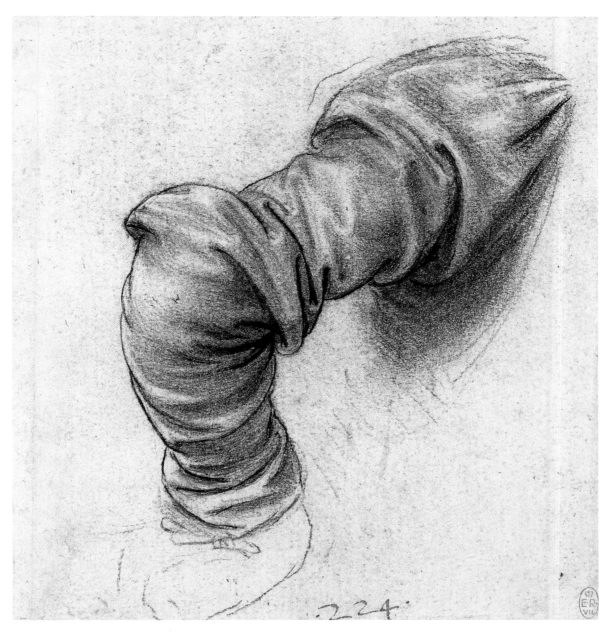

was not until the figures were knitted together on the wall that Leonardo accentuated the emotional keys upon which the power of the composition depends. In cat. 29 the face of the wizened old man registers merely mild surprise, not the dark look of horror of the painting; the youth of cat. 30 displays calm, if rapt, contemplation, whereas St Philip in the painting stares towards Christ in desperation.

Cat. 31 is the only drapery study for the *Last Supper* to survive. It shows St Peter's arm twisted behind his back as he leans over Judas's shoulder. The sense of inner life and the softness of handling of the black chalk – refined with white chalk and focussed with pen and ink – are unprecedented in Leonardo's work, and look forward to the drapery studies for the *St Anne* (cats. 78–80).

1500–1508
Mainly Florence

Our knowledge of Leonardo's activities during his first couple of years back in the city of his youth is scanty. The most precise information comes from two letters sent to Isabella d'Este in April 1501 by the head of the Carmelites in Florence, Fra Pietro da Novellara, regarding his continuing efforts to persuade Leonardo to execute something for Isabella's collection. He recorded that Leonardo had some obligation to the King of France; that he had two assistants who were painting portraits (or conceivably copies: *retrati*) with Leonardo's occasional intervention; that he was painting a *Madonna and Child* composition (see cat. 32) and working on a cartoon of the *Madonna and Child with St Anne and a lamb*; and that otherwise he was preoccupied with geometry and was "very impatient with the brush". Fra Pietro also noted that "Leonardo's life is changeful and very uncertain; it appears that he lives only for the day" – a glimpse of the inner life of the artist that we find all too rarely in his own notes.

Vasari (1550) recorded that Leonardo received a commission to paint the high altarpiece of Santissima Annunziata in Florence (this must have been in the first years of the century), but produced nothing for it and in the mean time executed a cartoon of the Madonna and Child with St Anne, a lamb and the infant Baptist. Vasari had not seen any of the three different versions of the *St Anne*; like all early writers on Leonardo, he assumed there was only one and conflated his information on the three versions, and thus his description does not tally with any surviving composition. But Fra Pietro's account fits perfectly with a composition known from a painting by Brescianino (destroyed, formerly Berlin, Kaiser-Friedrichs-Museum), which is probably a copy of the cartoon executed in Florence and, if Vasari is to be believed, exhibited there to great acclaim. The cartoon of the *Madonna and Child with St*

Detail of cat. 36

Anne and the infant Baptist, now in the National Gallery, London, seems not to have been known in Florence at this time. Padre Resta (died 1696) wrote of a cartoon of *St Anne* that had been ordered by the King of France from Leonardo before 1500, and although Resta is a very late source, the precise nature of his testimony is convincing and suggests that the National Gallery cartoon could have been executed in Milan towards the end of the 1490s.

Leonardo's impatience with the brush, attested by Fra Pietro, had the consequence of depriving him of any reliable source of income, for there was no opening for a court artist in republican Florence. Thus in the summer of 1502 he joined the entourage of Cesare Borgia, serving as his military architect until March 1503 (see p. 89). The reason for Leonardo's return to Florence – apart from the instability of life in the service of one who sailed as close to the wind as Cesare – may have been a request to execute the *Battle of Anghiari* (cats. 35–39). The date of the commission for this painting is not documented, but in October 1503 Leonardo was in a position to begin work on the cartoon.

Although the *Battle of Anghiari* was the most prestigious commission of Leonardo's career, that did not prevent him from being diverted on to other projects. In May 1504 he finally bowed to pressure from Isabella d'Este and accepted a commission to paint a young Christ (see cats. 43–44), though the painting was almost certainly never executed, at least by Leonardo himself. At around the same time he probably began the *Mona Lisa*, and was also working on compositions of *Neptune*, the *Angel of the Annunciation* (see cat. 39) and *Leda and the swan* (cats. 40–42); and during 1504 Leonardo's engineering skills were called upon at least twice by the Republic – in

the summer he was consulted about a scheme to divert the Arno at Pisa (see cat. 53), and that November he was at Piombino, on the coast south of Livorno, advising on fortifications.

During 1505 most of Leonardo's efforts were concentrated on the painting of the *Battle of Anghiari*, though he still found time to compile manuscripts on the flight of birds (Turin) and stereometry (Forster I). The last document referring to his work on the *Battle* is from October of that year, and in May 1506 Leonardo obtained leave to return to Milan for three months, to work for the French occupiers of the city. This marked the start of an unsettled two years for Leonardo, during which he travelled between Florence and Milan at least five times. First his leave was extended until the end of September 1506, after the governor of Milan, Charles d'Amboise, wrote to the Florentine Signoria of a "certain work that he has started", perhaps a painting or an architectural project (see cat. 58). In October the Signoria requested Leonardo's immediate return, but their request was ignored, and he remained in Milan until at least January 1507.

The same month, the Florentine ambassador in France wrote to the Signoria that Louis XII wished to have Leonardo in his service. The king took a personal interest in Leonardo; as mentioned above, the London *St Anne* cartoon may have been commissioned by Louis shortly after the occupation of Milan, and Vasari claimed that the king had tried to find a way to transport the *Last Supper* to France. Working in Milan, Leonardo was an official painter and engineer to the king by 26 July 1507, when a letter was sent to the Signoria requesting a rapid settlement of litigation between Leonardo and his half-brothers over the will of an uncle.

Leonardo returned to Florence to

settle this business in August 1507, and stayed there until the following spring. Oddly, there is no evidence that he resumed work on the *Battle of Anghiari*, although this was presumably the reason for the Signoria's repeated requests for Leonardo's return to the city. Instead he claimed in a letter to the French in Milan to have worked on "two Madonnas of different sizes which I have commenced for the most Christian king or for whosoever you wish"; these cannot now be identified, and the sentence implies that they were not executed to commission.

Leonardo also occupied himself in Florence by returning to a sustained study of human anatomy. In the winter of 1507–08 he performed an autopsy on an old man in the hospital of Santa Maria Nuova, and the resulting drawings (including cat. 48) are the most extensive record of a single dissection by Leonardo to survive. This was to be the basis of his greatest achievements in anatomy, after his decisive return to Milan around Easter 1508.

32

A study of the bust of a woman

ca. 1499–1501
Metalpoint underdrawing, red chalk on orange-red prepared paper
221 x 159 mm (8¹¹⁄₁₆″ x 6¼″)
No watermark
RL 12514

This drawing is a study for the bust of the Virgin in a painting known as the *Madonna of the Yarnwinder*, in progress by 14 April 1501 when the head of the Carmelites in Florence, Fra Pietro da Novellara, wrote to Isabella d'Este about his continuing efforts to persuade Leonardo to execute something for her collection. He described a painting for the Secretary to King Louis XII, Florimond Robertet, whom Leonardo had probably met when the French occupied Milan in 1499: "The little picture which he is doing is of a Madonna seated as if she were about to spin yarn. The Child has placed His foot on the basket of yarns and has grasped the yarnwinder and gazes attentively at the four spokes that are in the form of a cross. As if desirous of the cross He smiles and holds it firm, and is unwilling to yield it to His mother who seems to want to take it away from Him." Besides the psychological interplay, this sophisticated painting combined a foreshadowing of the Passion, in the shape of the yarnwinder and Christ's eager grasping of it, with an allusion to the Madonna's antetype, Eve, who was occasionally depicted spinning wool after the Expulsion from Paradise, the infants Cain and Abel at her lap. The iconography thus encompasses the Fall, mankind's subsequent travails, and our redemption through Christ's sacrifice.

Of the many surviving versions of the painting, two are notably superior in execution, those in the collection of the Duke of Buccleuch (fig. 7) and in a private collection in New York. The best

Fig. 7
Attributed to Leonardo da Vinci and assistant, *The Madonna of the Yarnwinder*
Oil on panel, 48.3 x 36.9 cm (19″ x 14½″). In the collection of the Duke of Buccleuch, KT

passages of the Buccleuch painting do seem acceptable as by Leonardo himself, though much of the landscape is clumsy. It was argued by Martin Kemp in a recent exhibition, where the two paintings were placed side by side for the first time this century (Edinburgh, 1992), that both were produced in Leonardo's workshop, the Buccleuch painting being the primary version for Robertet (though not completely autograph), the New York version executed by a workshop assistant under Leonardo's guidance; the essence of this reconstruction of events is probably correct.

In these paintings the Madonna's drapery and the angle of her shoulders are not as shown in cat. 32, and the drawing has also been claimed as a study for the portrait of Cecilia Gallerani, or even for the Louvre *St Anne*. That the drawing is a study for the *Yarnwinder* is proved by a sheet in the Accademia, Venice, in the same technique but probably a copy by Cesare da Sesto after a lost study by Leonardo very similar to cat. 32. This shows the Madonna bust-length with the face completed and, in the left margin, four quick sketches of the Madonna, in one of which she is seated and holds her right hand in the distinctive pose of the *Yarnwinder* composition.

Cat. 32 appears to be one of the latest examples in Leonardo's career of the use of metalpoint, visible in the facial features, but it is possible that in other sheets of the period metalpoint was used for the underdrawing; in the bust of the figure here any underdrawing is obscured by the red chalk, handled with a freedom and assurance typical of Leonardo in the first decade of the century.

33

A tree

ca. 1502
Red chalk, touched with a damp brush
191 x 153 mm (7½″ x 6″)
No watermark
RL 12431v

The drawings on the two sides of this sheet are among the most sensitive and atmospheric of Leonardo's career. This delicacy was achieved in part by touching the red chalk with a wet brush, to soften the outlines and create a continuous range of tones. There is a deliberate contrast between the left side of the tree, in shadow and flatly rendered, and the illuminated right side, showing the clumps of foliage in relief, as explained by the block of text below: *That part of a tree which is against shadow is all of one tone, and where the density of trees and branches is greater, there it is darker because light has less of an impression there. But where the branches are against other branches, there the luminous parts show themselves brighter, and the leaves shine as the sun illuminates them.*

This is the type of statement found throughout Leonardo's writings in preparation for his planned treatise on painting. The Codex Urbinas, a compilation transcribed from his notebooks by Francesco Melzi in an attempt to piece together the never completed treatise, contains many more observations of similar complexity on the optical properties of trees.

The sheet is difficult to date on grounds of style alone. A similarly conceived group of trees in red chalk (though without the use of a damp brush) is found in Paris MS. L (f. 81v) opposite a note on Cesena, which Leonardo visited in the service of Cesare Borgia in 1502, and it is quite possible that cat. 33 dates from the same period.

34

A seated youth, and a child with a lamb

ca. 1503–06
Black chalk
173 x 140 mm (6¹³⁄₁₆″ x 5½″)
No watermark
RL 12540

The drawing of a seated youth on this sheet is Leonardo's closest copy after an ancient work of art. It is based on the figure of Diomedes in a famous antique gem, reputedly found around the neck of a boy in the streets of Florence. The gem, a chalcedony intaglio, passed through the hands of Niccolò Niccoli, Pope Paul II and Lorenzo de' Medici before its loss in consequence of the flight from Florence of Lorenzo's son Piero in 1494. The composition was widely circulated during the fifteenth century and beyond through replicas and adaptations, including a large marble tondo by the workshop of Donatello in the courtyard of the Palazzo Medici (fig. 8).

Leonardo has stripped the figure of its drapery and attribute, the sacred statuette known as the Palladium, held by Diomedes in his left hand; the identity of the youth, and thus the significance of the statuette, was not known in the Renaissance. The pose of the left arm was altered into an upwards-pointing gesture, which, with the figure's youth, led Clark to suggest that it might have been intended for a Baptist in the Wilderness, though the Baptist ought to gesture with his right hand. The Florentine associations of the Diomedes figure would indicate a (stylistically acceptable) date of around 1503–06.

The separate motif of the Child wrestling with a lamb also occurs on a sheet of pen-and-ink studies in the J. Paul Getty Museum of about the same date, and in three painted variants of a *Madonna with the infants Christ and St John*

(Ashmolean; Uffizi; Gallerati Scotti collection). However, the posture of the Madonna in that composition originated in a drawing of the early 1480s (Metropolitan Museum, New York, P. 159). This suggests two possibilities: the Child with the lamb in cat. 34 is a reprise of a motif invented twenty years earlier, and the paintings reflect a composition by Leonardo from the 1480s; or the paintings are pastiches of Leonardesque components from different stages of his career. Either would be acceptable on the available evidence. The Child with the lamb has also been linked to the *St Anne* project (see cats. 75–80), but this connection is supported only by the general iconography and not by the particulars of the pose.

Fig. 8 Workshop of Donatello, *Diomedes*
Marble. Florence, Palazzo Medici-Riccardi

The Battle of Anghiari

35
A body of cavalry

ca. 1503–04. Black chalk, 160 x 197 mm
(6⁵⁄₁₆″ x 7¾″). No watermark
RL 12339

Fig. 9
Peter Paul Rubens, after Leonardo
The fight for the standard, black chalk, pen and
ink, wash, white and grey bodycolour,
452 x 637 mm (17¹³⁄₁₆″ x 25¹⁄₁₆″).
Paris, Musée du Louvre

36
A galloping horse, and other sketches

ca. 1503–04. Red chalk, 168 x 240 mm
(6⁵⁄₈″ x 9⁷⁄₁₆″), irregular. No watermark
RL 12340

37
A rearing horse

ca. 1503–04. Black chalk, 131 x 127 mm
(5³⁄₁₆″ x 5″), irregular. No watermark
RL 12334

38
A horse's head

ca. 1503–04. Pen and ink with wash,
108 x 61 mm (4¼″ x 2⅜″). No watermark
RL 12327

39
Sketches of horses, the Angel of the Annunciation, etc

ca. 1503–04. Black chalk, and pen and ink,
210 x 283 mm (8¼″ x 11⅛″), upper left corner
torn, lower corners cut. No watermark
RL 12328

cat. 35

cat. 36

Probably some time around the middle of 1503, Leonardo agreed to paint a huge mural of the *Battle of Anghiari* in the Sala del Gran Consiglio of the Palazzo della Signoria in Florence; the following year, a pendant, the *Battle of Cascina*, was commissioned from his young rival, Michelangelo. The Sala del Gran Consiglio, conceived after the expulsion of the Medici in 1494, was to have been the showpiece of the Florentine Republic, designed and decorated by the finest Florentine artists and craftsmen of the day. Each of the two huge paintings was to represent a celebrated military victory of the Republic: the battle of Cascina against Pisa in 1364, the battle of Anghiari against Milan in 1440, when the Florentines in league with papal forces held a strategic bridge over the Tiber at Anghiari in eastern Tuscany, thus driving the Milanese back towards Borgo San Sepolcro.

On 24 October 1503 Leonardo was given the keys to the Sala del Papa of Santa Maria Novella, a room big enough to prepare the full-scale cartoon for the painting. A revised contract of 4 May 1504 stipulated a deadline of February 1505 either for completion of the cartoon, or for the start of work on that portion of the mural for which the cartoon had been completed. Leonardo evidently chose the latter option, for he began to make preparations for the painting in the Palazzo della Signoria that summer, a process which was hampered by his hydrographic work for the Republic (see cats. 54–57) and a spell as military engineer to Jacopo Appiani at Piombino in November 1504. As the February 1505 deadline passed, plaster and other preparatory materials were still being ordered. By April 1505, Leonardo had finally begun to paint the mural, with two assistants, and the last record we have of his work on the commission is an

cat. 37

order for more materials that October. In May 1506 he was called back to Milan, and, much to the chagrin of the government of Florence, he never returned to the project.

Only a portion of the centre of the painting, showing the *Fight for the standard*, was completed, and this was widely copied before its replacement by Vasari's frescos after 1563 (but the most sympathetic version, usually attributed to Rubens, cannot have been done from the original; fig. 9). Speculative reconstructions of the remainder of the design are compromised by the probability that Leonardo did not execute a cartoon for the flanking episodes, for the contract allowed him to begin the painting without completing the entire cartoon; thus there would be no final design to reconstruct.

We can, however, get a good idea of Leonardo's intentions for the right side of the mural from cat. 35, the most carefully drawn of the surviving compositional studies. This shows a group of cavalry on a low hill, waiting to move away and down to the left to cross the bridge and join the main battle at the centre of the painting; one horse can be seen galloping away at the left of the sheet, and a light line where the drawing stops abruptly indicates the right edge of the whole composition. A sheet by Raphael in the Ashmolean Museum, Oxford, which includes sketches after both the *Fight for the standard* and the horse seen from behind in the present drawing, has been taken as proof that the right side of the composition also reached the cartoon stage, but it seems that Raphael had access to some of Leonardo's drawings around these years (see cat. 40), and his copy may have been made after sheets such as cat. 35 rather than after the cartoon.

Cat. 36 is preparatory for the left side of the mural, about which little is known

(a drawing by Michelangelo in the British Museum has been claimed as a copy after this portion of the putative whole cartoon, but there is no real evidence for this). The furiously galloping horse appears in other studies for the painting, including cat. 39, and would presumably have been one of the terminal elements at the far left of the composition. Along the lower left edge of the sheet is a very rapid sketch of a kicking horse, also found again on cat. 39. This motif is one of the most memorable in Uccello's *Rout of San Romano* panels, the finest Florentine battle cycle of the fifteenth century, then in the Palazzo Medici and presumably accessible to Leonardo during the Republic. At upper left are three studies of a man apparently preparing to deliver a slashing blow with a sword; neither he nor the kicking horse can be identified in any of Leonardo's compositional sketches for the mural. The drawings are among Leonardo's loosest in red chalk, a medium he normally reserved for careful and controlled studies.

Cat. 37 examines one of Leonardo's favourite poses for a horse, rearing and twisting its neck violently backwards. The horse can be seen, with a rider, to the right of the *Fight for the standard* group in one of the small pen-and-ink sketches for the mural (Venice, Accademia), but did not survive the refinement of the group into its final, highly compressed form. The motif first appears in Leonardo's work twenty-five years earlier, in the drawings of a dragon fight and the related combat scene in the background of the *Adoration of the Magi*, and was used in the right foreground of the study for the presentation drawing of *Neptune* (RL 12570), *ca.* 1503–04. The present sheet is a clarification of a sketch on RL 12336, where the horse is shown with its head in at least three different positions; the rear quarters are studied again on RL 12335, in

cat. 38

cat. 39

which a saddle is drawn.

Cat. 38 constitutes background research for the *Battle of Anghiari*, as Leonardo with his characteristic thoroughness gathered raw material for the composition – a list of his books made around this time includes "a book of horses sketched for the cartoon" (Madrid MS. II f. 3r). This is the most intricately worked of a number of studies of horses' heads made in connection with the *Battle*, showing the beetling brow and flared nostrils of extreme exertion. Leonardo wished to convey the passion of battle through the expressions as well as through the poses of the participants, both man and beast; cat. 38 is a fragment of a sheet (RL 12326) on which Leonardo compared the looks of fury of horses, a man and a lion, but as far as we know, none was used directly in the cartoon.

Cat. 39 is the most varied sheet connected with the *Battle of Anghiari*. Many of the small pen-and-ink sketches are studies for the composition, most obvi-

ously the horses (though one, at lower centre, is a partial copy after an antique coin, with the profile of Nero from the obverse of the same coin immediately to the right). More interesting are the sketches below and to the left of the centre of the sheet, which show men pole-vaulting across a ditch. These are probably first thoughts for the foreground between the central and right-hand groups, separated by the river, and give our only indication of how Leonardo planned to integrate these two sections of the composition, for the vital bridge was necessarily in the background, to avoid depicting it on an oppressively large scale. A note at lower centre reminds Leonardo to "make a little one out of wax, one finger long", suggesting that he used small wax models to help orchestrate the composition of the *Battle*.

The standing nude at the centre left of the sheet is strongly reminiscent of Michelangelo's *David*. Leonardo was a member of the committee which met on

Detail of cat. 39

25 January 1504 to decide where the sculpture, then almost complete, ought to be placed (see cat. 58), and the identity of style with the *Anghiari* sketches would indicate that Leonardo's memento of the statue was drawn at about this time.

The large *Angel of the Annunciation* to the right was the first drawing to be added to the sheet. The black chalk is weak and shaded with the right hand, and must be a copy by a pupil of Leonardo, though the master corrected the too-thin right arm in ink. A painting of this subject reputedly by Leonardo was recorded by Vasari (1568) in the collection of Duke Cosimo de' Medici; no original is now known, but several versions by other hands have survived (*e.g.* fig. 10). The painting is not documented, but this drawing demonstrates that the design had been worked out by 1504 at the latest.

Fig. 10 Copy after Leonardo da Vinci, *The Angel of the Annunciation*
Oil on panel, 71 x 52 cm (27¹⁵⁄₁₆″ x 20⁷⁄₁₆″). Basle, Öffentliche Kunstsammlung

Leda and the swan

40

The head of Leda

ca. 1505–07
Black-chalk underdrawing, pen and ink
177 x 147 mm (6¹⁵⁄₁₆″ x 5¹³⁄₁₆″)
Watermark: tulip, close to Briquet 6664
RL 12518

41

A Star of Bethlehem, with crowsfoot and wood anemone

ca. 1505–07
Red chalk and pen and ink
198 x 160 mm (7¹³⁄₁₆″ x 6⁵⁄₁₆″)
Watermark: bull's head, not in Briquet
RL 12424

42

A bramble

ca. 1505–07
Red chalk, touches of white chalk, on pale orange-red prepared paper
155 x 162 mm (6⅛″ x 6⅜″)
Watermark: eight-petalled flower (cut), in range Briquet 6596–97, 6599–603
RL 12419

Leda, the wife of Tyndareus, King of Sparta, was seduced by Jupiter in the form of a swan and bore two eggs, from which hatched Helen of Troy, Clytemnestra, and Castor and Pollux. Leonardo worked on two variants of a composition of Leda with the swan, one in which the woman kneels, the other in which she stands. The kneeling version was under way by 1504, when Leonardo sketched the contorted figure three times on a sheet (RL 12337) that also contains a study for the *Battle of Anghiari*; two further, fully resolved, compositions of the kneeling Leda survive in drawings at Chatsworth (fig. 11) and Rotterdam (P. 208). The pose of Leda in these two drawings, of extreme contrivance and instability, was apparently abandoned without a cartoon or painting being made, and Leonardo turned instead to a composition with Leda standing. A carefully worked drawing, if not a full-scale version, was completed by 1508 at the latest, for it was copied by Raphael before he left Florence for Rome that year (fig. 12).

The style of cat. 40, and of three other studies of Leda's head for the standing version (RL 12515–17), points to a date of around 1505–07, when Leonardo's use of curvilinear modelling was fully developed (cf. cat. 39, of *ca.* 1503–04). A *terminus ante quem* of 1507 for these drawings is provided by another sheet by Raphael, in the British Museum, preparatory for his *Borghese Christ carried to the tomb* of that year, which includes sketches of elaborate hairstyles that betray knowledge of the Leda head studies.

Fig. 11
Leonardo da Vinci, *Leda and the swan*
Black-chalk underdrawing, pen and ink, wash, 160 x 139 mm (6⁵⁄₁₆″ x 5½″)
Chatsworth, Devonshire Collection

The fantastic and somewhat distracting *coiffures* seen in this series of drawings for the standing Leda conform to Leonardo's love of personal beauty and ornamentation, which found fertile expression in the costumes for court entertainments that he was called upon to devise throughout his life (cats. 88–93). Indeed one of the studies (RL 12515) carries the curious note, "this kind can be taken off and put on without being damaged", implying that Leonardo envisaged Leda wearing a wig.

Apparently Leonardo did not progress with the standing Leda for some years after 1508 – the next time we find him considering the composition is around 1514–15, in a sketch in the Codex Atlanticus (f. 156r–b). But he did finally execute a painting of the subject, which was the most highly valued item in an inventory of the estate of Leonardo's assistant Salaì after the latter's death in 1524. The painting was seen by Cassiano dal Pozzo at Fontainebleau in 1625, but its deteriorating condition seems to have led to its destruction some time between 1694 and 1775. Several painted copies of the composition are known, which agree generally in the forms of Leda and the swan but differ greatly in the backgrounds, suggesting that some of the copies were made from a cartoon in which the background was barely indicated, rather than from the finished panel.

Alongside his studies of the figure of Leda, Leonardo worked assiduously on incidental details for the composition, primarily a series of botanical drawings at Windsor (RL 12419–30; 12426 and 12428 are copies). Plants studied by Leonardo in this series occur in several different combinations in the painted copies, for which the only simple explanation is that many of them were used by Leonardo in his cartoon and painting, whereas his less diligent followers selected just a few plants from the original for

their own versions – we know from the surviving decoration in the Sala delle Asse of the Castello Sforzesco in Milan, and from Vasari's description of a lost cartoon for a tapestry of Adam and Eve, that Leonardo would occasionally indulge in luxuriant organic decoration.

Several of the botanical studies, such as cat. 42, are executed on orange-red prepared paper, and are as objective and delicate as any scientific drawing produced during Leonardo's career. Two of these (cat. 42 and RL 12422) bear folds and matching stitch-marks, and it is possible that all come from a single sketchbook made up by Leonardo from prepared paper. The studies on unprepared paper (including cat. 41) are more stylized and approach the artificiality of the studies of Leda herself. Plants of a swirling form very similar to that of cat. 41 can be seen in the foreground of both the Chatsworth and Rotterdam drawings for the kneeling version, and are found in some of the many copied variants of the standing Leda. The beautifully patterned arrangement of the leaves of the *Star of Bethlehem* seen here is far from natural; Leonardo's approach to the drawing parallels his studies of human anatomy around this time, in which he would synthesize direct observation of detail with a premeditated perception of underlying structure.

Emphasizing the recurrence of certain forms, in particular the vortex, has become something of a cliché of commentaries on Leonardo's work, but it is central to an understanding of his response to the myth of Leda, where the twisting forms permeate all of visible Creation – woman, swan, children, plants – with the same sense of fertility. The composition was worked on at a time when Leonardo was increasingly fascinated by the processes of life – culminating in his dissection of the "centenarian" in the winter of 1507–08 (see cat. 48).

Fig. 12
Raphael, after Leonardo
Leda and the swan
Stylus underdrawing, pen and ink,
308 x 192 mm (12⅛" x 7⁹⁄₁₆")
RL 12759

cat. 40

cat. 41

cat. 42

The Salvator Mundi

43
Studies of drapery

ca. 1504–08
Upper drawing: red chalk with touches of
white chalk; lower drawing: red chalk with
touches of black chalk, and white heightening;
on orange-red prepared paper
164 x 158 mm (6⁷⁄₁₆″ x 6¼″)
No watermark
RL 12525

44
A study of drapery

ca. 1504–08
Red chalk with touches of black and white
chalks on orange-red prepared paper
220 x 139 mm (8¹¹⁄₁₆″ x 5½″)
No watermark
RL 12524

Cats. 43 and 44 are studies for the drapery
over the chest and right arm in a painting of *Christ as Salvator Mundi*, holding a
crystal globe and blessing the spectator, a
type of devotional picture popular in both
Italy and northern Europe during the
fifteenth and early sixteenth centuries.
No painting of the subject by Leonardo
survives; the composition is known from
an etching of 1650 by Wenceslaus Hollar
(fig. 13) after a painting then thought to
be by the hand of Leonardo, and from a
number of painted versions, some of
which have been optimistically claimed as
autograph.

The subject of the *Salvator Mundi*
would have been most uncongenial to
Leonardo, forcing him to work to an
iconic formula that presented no formal
challenge or psychological tensions.
Cats. 43 and 44 are unusually coarse in
handling: the initial outlines appear far
too imprecise to be by Leonardo, and
although the modelling in red chalk is
drawn with the left hand and is of high
enough quality to pass as his, the crude

white heightening of cat. 43 is hatched
with the right hand and must have been
added by an assistant. The technique is
that of the first decade of the sixteenth
century, when we know that Leonardo
had assistants working in his studio (see
cat. 32), and it is quite possible that in
some cases he prepared designs specific-
ally for execution by his assistants. Therefore the prime version of the *Salvator
Mundi* need not have been by Leonardo
himself.

In May 1504, a painting of "a youthful
Christ of around twelve years, which
would be of that age that He had when
He disputed in the Temple" was requested from Leonardo by the importunate
Isabella d'Este. It is unlikely that Leonardo
himself ever executed a painting of that
subject, but a heavily Leonardesque composition of *Christ among the Doctors* that
survives in a number of versions (for
instance that by Bernardino Luini in the
National Gallery, London) may depend,
in the figure of Christ, on a design by
Leonardo intended for Isabella. The
composition of the *Salvator Mundi* is a
variant of this, showing Christ as fully
mature and divested of any narrative context, and must therefore be datable to
some time after 1504. At least three of the
surviving versions have a French provenance, and it is possible that the painting
was one of the projects pressed upon
Leonardo after he was called back to
Milan by the occupying French court in
1506 (though the elaborate historical
reconstruction put forward by Snow-
Smith in 1982 is wildly speculative).

Fig. 13
Wenceslaus Hollar, after Leonardo
Christ as Salvator Mundi, etching,
251 x 174 mm (9⅞″ x 6⅞″)

45
The anatomy of a male nude,
and a battle scene

ca. 1504–06
Red chalk, and pen and ink
160 x 152 mm (6⁵⁄₁₆″ x 6″)
Watermark: bull's head (cut), not in Briquet
RL 12640

The small battle group (many other figures are loosely sketched in behind the
three main combatants) is reminiscent of
Leonardo's pen-and-ink studies for the
Battle of Anghiari, but there is no strong
connection with the known motifs of that
composition; the sketch could be connected just as easily with a number of later
drawings of tiny figures in action,
whether at work (RL 12643–46 etc,
ca. 1506–08) or in combat (RL 12332,
ca. 1511).

The anatomical drawings are a development of Leonardo's studies of superficial anatomy that sprang from work on
the *Anghiari* project. Here he examined

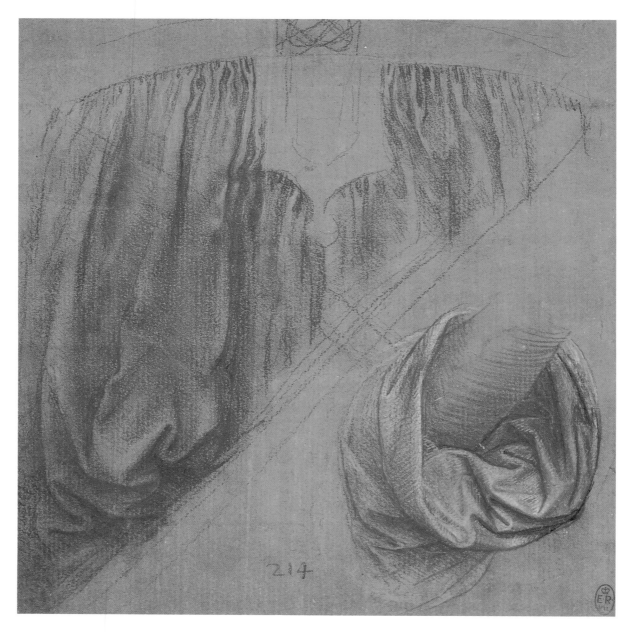

cat. 43

cat. 44

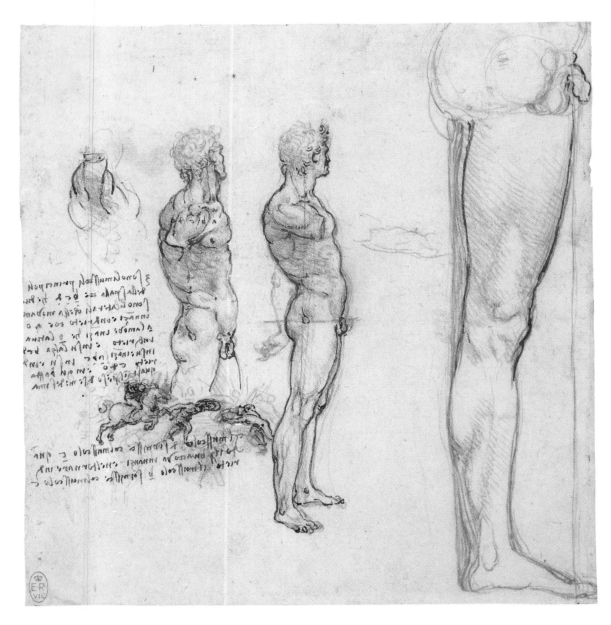

cat. 45

the action of individual muscles, but his findings were apparently not yet based on human dissection, thus dating the sheet to before the centenarian dissection of the winter of 1507–08 (see cat. 48). Leonardo had no knowledge of the importance of latissimus dorsi and the deeper muscles arising from the scapula in the motions of the arm (*cf.* cat. 68). The three drawings to the left therefore show only the superficial muscles of the upper torso with the arm held upwards, backwards and forwards. The accompanying note states: *The principal muscles of the shoulder are three, that is,* b c d*; and there are two lateral ones that move it forwards and backwards, that is* a o*.* a *[pectoralis major] moves it forwards, and* o *[posterior digitation of the deltoid] pulls it backwards, and* b c d *[central digitations of the deltoid] upwards.*

46

The myology of the male torso, from the side

ca. 1506–08
Black-chalk underdrawing, pen and ink
192 x 140 mm (7⁹⁄₁₆″ x 5½″)
No watermark
RL 19032v

This is a page from the so called Anatomical MS. B, a notebook that Leonardo commenced in 1489 with a series of studies of the skull (including cats. 20–21), then abandoned for over fifteen years until his active interest in anatomy was revived in the wake of the *Anghiari* project.

As in cat. 45, Leonardo has 'amputated' the arm of his subject to show the superficial muscles of the torso, in particular the interdigitation of serratus anterior and the external oblique muscles. The arm lopped off at the shoulder is reminiscent of a damaged piece of ancient sculpture, and in this context should be read the cryptic note by

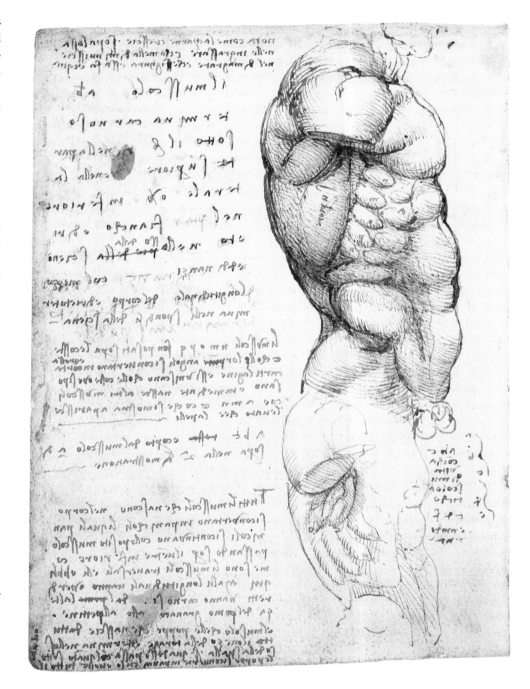

the two squiggles at lower right: a b c: *concavity of antique muscle; c d f is modern.* This refers to what Leonardo perceived as the contrast between antique and modern sculpture – the sharp dip in the upper line represents the exaggeratedly distinct outlines of the muscles in heroic antique statuary, a fashion that he also identified – and deplored – in some contemporaries "who, in order to appear to be great draftsmen, make their nudes wooden and without grace, so they seem a sack full of nuts rather than the surface of a human being" (MS. L f. 79).

47

The brachial plexus

ca. 1507
Black-chalk underdrawing, pen and ink
191 x 137 mm (7½″ x 5⅜″)
No watermark
RL 19040

Cat. 47 displays the second and third of a sequence of four highly schematized diagrams of the brachial plexus, the network of nerves between the neck and the arm. The upper drawing shows the cervical vertebrae 'sawn through' to reveal a central and two lateral nerve cords; in the lower drawing the bones are removed, leaving the nerves and the base of the brain exposed. The drawings are very inaccurate, both in the structure of the spinal cord and in the configuration of the plexus, and it may be that, unconsciously, the diagrammatic simplifications conceal Leonardo's inadequate understanding of this complicated region.

Another drawing of the brachial plexus from Anatomical MS. B (RL 19020v) shows the area much more accurately. Like the drawings in cat. 48 it is labelled *del vechio* (of the old man), indicating that it was based on Leonardo's dissection of the centenarian in the winter of 1507–08. Even during the winter, without fixative or preservative, Leonardo would have had little time after the death – a couple of days at most – to dissect the body, and he must have known what he was looking for to obtain such a quantity of accurate information. It is therefore probable that the present sheet, showing only partial understanding, dates from 1507 or shortly before, and served as the basis for Leonardo's dissection of the centenarian's shoulder.

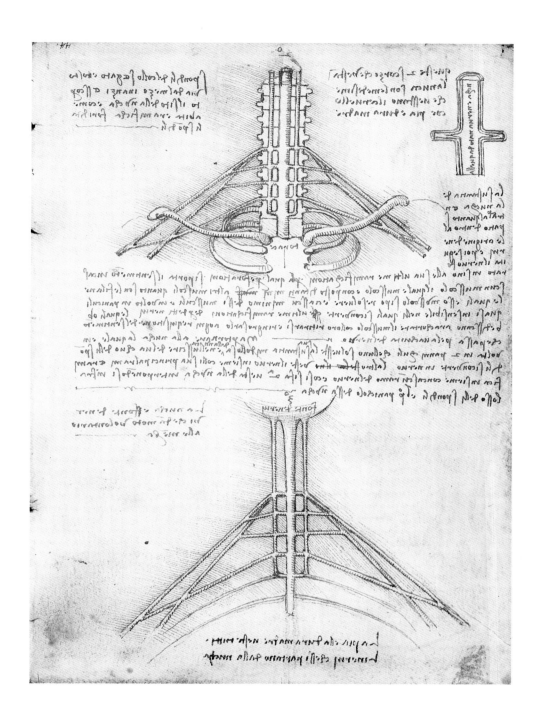

48

The vessels of the liver

ca. 1508
Black-chalk underdrawing, pen and ink
190 x 137 mm (7½″ x 5⅜″), left side shaped
No watermark
RL 19051v

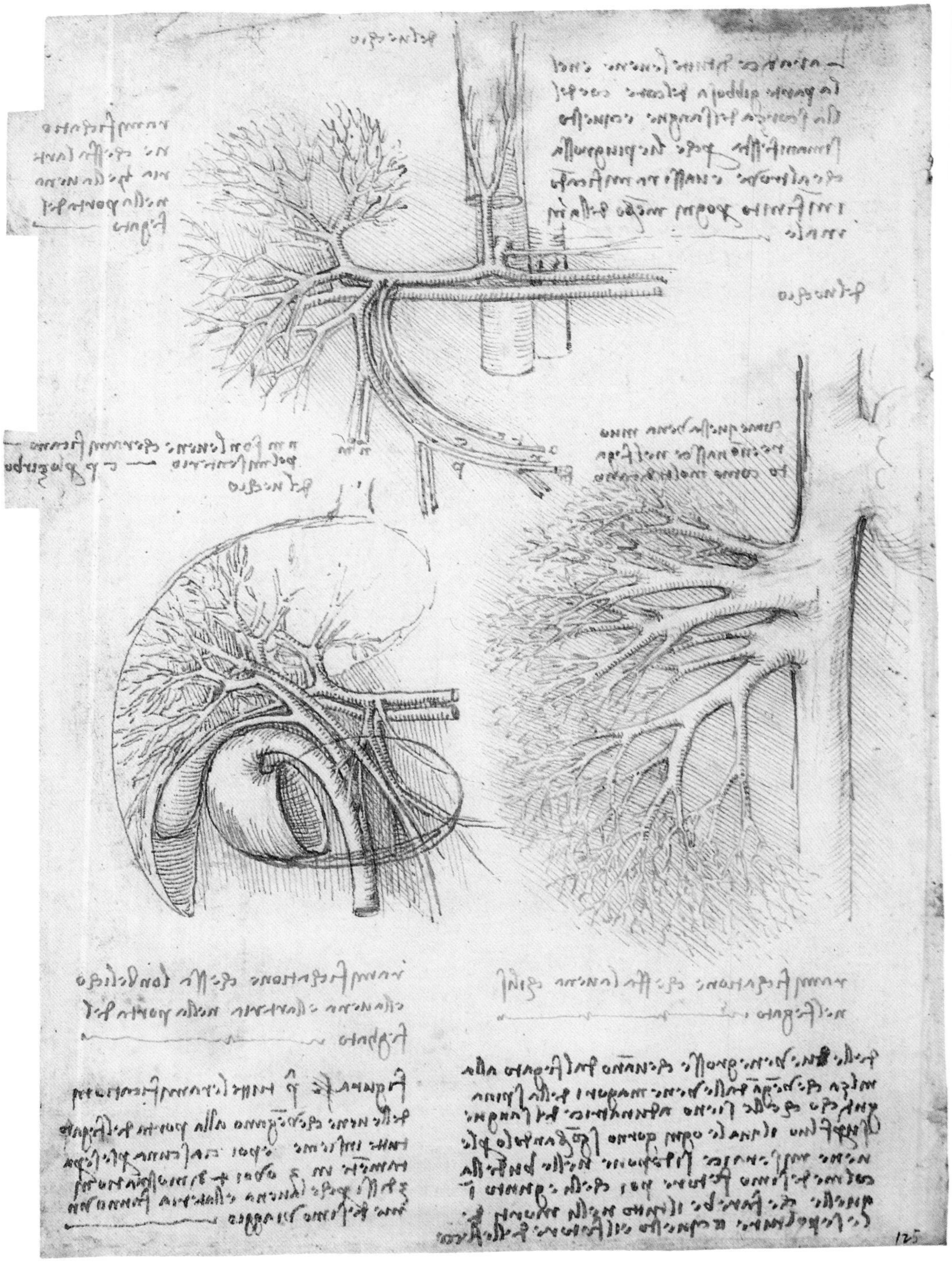

In the winter of 1507–08 Leonardo witnessed the peaceful death of a man "over a hundred years old" in the hospital attached to the monastery of Santa Maria Nuova in Florence, and he performed a dissection "to see the cause of so sweet a death". He recorded for the first time in medical history cirrhosis of the liver, arteriosclerosis, calcification of the vessels, and coronary vascular occlusion (RL 19027v). Further, "the absence of fat and humours which greatly hinder the recognition of the parts" allowed Leonardo to perform his single most extensive dissection of the vessels and viscera of a human.

The actual dissection notes, which would inevitably have been soiled, have not survived; what we have are the fair copies made by Leonardo in the Anatomical MS. B, where he clarified and expanded his observations, probably a few months later, after his return to Milan in the spring of 1508. Each of the three diagrams on cat. 48 is headed *del vechio* (of the old man), and is therefore based on the observations made during the dissection of the centenarian.

The upper diagram concentrates on the coeliac trunk arising from the aorta, showing the left gastric, splenic and hepatic branches, though the last two appear to form a continuous vessel from liver to spleen. Several identifiable arteries branch away below, each with an accompanying (though inaccurately drawn) vein. The diagram at lower right depicts the intralobular and sublobular stages of the hepatic veins converging on the inferior vena cava, which passes into the right atrium of the heart, described by Leonardo above as *the root of all the veins*. The third diagram shows more accurately the ramifications within the liver, as well as the gall bladder, the cystic duct and artery, the hepatic ducts, the common bile duct, and the (cirrhotically enlarged) umbilical vein.

1502–1504
Leonardo's maps

Leonardo entered the service of Cesare Borgia, the illegitimate son of Pope Alexander VI and also the model for Macchiavelli's *The Prince*, some time during the summer of 1502. Leonardo had probably met him for the first time in 1499, after Cesare had entered Milan at the shoulder of Louis XII. A Marshal of the Papal Troops, and recently created Duke of Romagna by his father and Duke of Valentinois by the French king, he was rapidly increasing his influence over much of the territory bordering the Florentine state. The Republic therefore made him a *condottiere* with an annual payment of 30,000 gold ducats, effectively protection money, and Macchiavelli was sent on a diplomatic mission to Cesare's court in June 1502. It was possibly then that Leonardo's services were offered as a further sweetener from the Florentines, for we find the artist in Cesare's entourage at Urbino the following month.

On 18 August Leonardo was granted the title of *Architecto et Ingegnero Generale* to Cesare, giving him and his companions access to all Borgia strongholds, freedom to order any improvements to fortifications, and powers to requisition men for surveying duties. For the rest of the year Leonardo toured Emilia and the Marches, and his MS. L records visits to Cesena, Rimini, Urbino, Pesaro and Imola, where a magnificent map of the town, cat. 50, was made.

Although Leonardo is not documented in Cesare's service after October 1502, a note about Siena suggests that he remained with him until at least January 1503, when the city was taken by Borgia. On 4 March 1503 Leonardo withdrew money from his account in Santa Maria Nuova, which probably indicates that he had returned to Florence. But he continued to make maps for over a year: some are connected with his dreams of building a canal from Florence towards the sea, by-passing much of the Arno (cats. 54–55); others were probably commissioned by the Republic, including accurate maps of the area around Pisa connected with the siege of that city in 1503-04, and surveys of the Arno east and west of Florence (cats. 56–57), perhaps required as part of a scheme to maintain the river banks and thus minimize the effects of the Arno's frequent floods.

The large-scale maps made around this time were evidently surveyed by Leonardo himself, for we have preparatory drawings, cats. 49 and 56, and the accuracy of the end-products testifies to the soundness of his method. But the maps that cover large tracts of countryside (cats. 51–55) cannot have been based solely on personal measurement, and Leonardo must have been dependent upon earlier maps for the general layout of towns and rivers, as he was demonstrably for cat. 51. Then he could be only as accurate as his model, and in some cases, such as cats. 52–53, the difference between Leonardo's drawing and his prototype, over most of the area covered, can have amounted to nothing more substantial than the beauty of Leonardo's handling of his materials. But occasionally he would transform the cartographic conventions of the era, modelling the landscape with wash in cat. 51, and even employing a genuine contour line on a map of the Arno valley in the Madrid MS. II. These innovations give some of his maps of large areas the same sense of objectivity as his surveys of Imola and the stretches of the Arno; it is this conception of a map as a scientific record, rather than an accumulation of incidental detail, that is the essence of Leonardo's achievement as a cartographer.

Detail of cat. 53

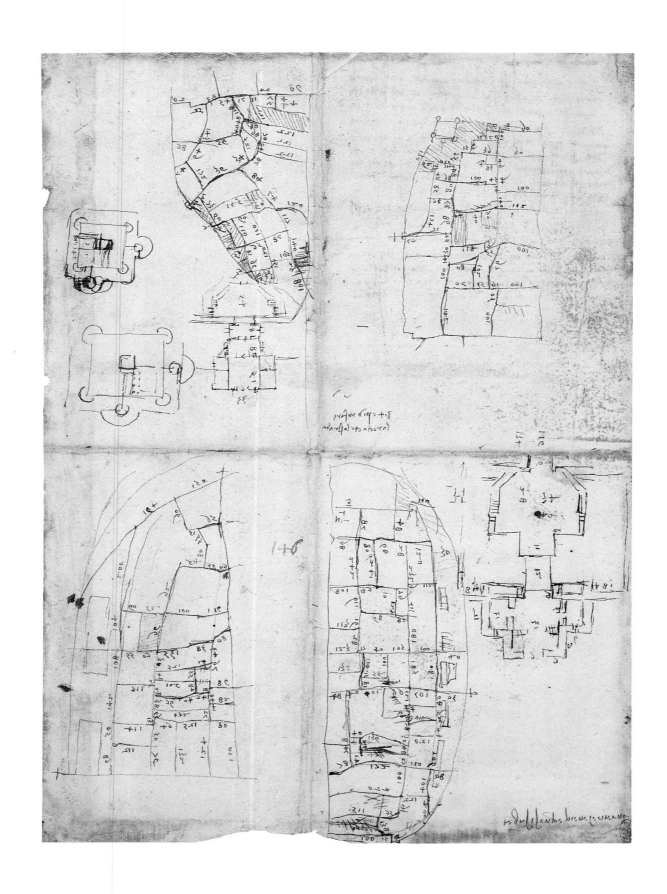

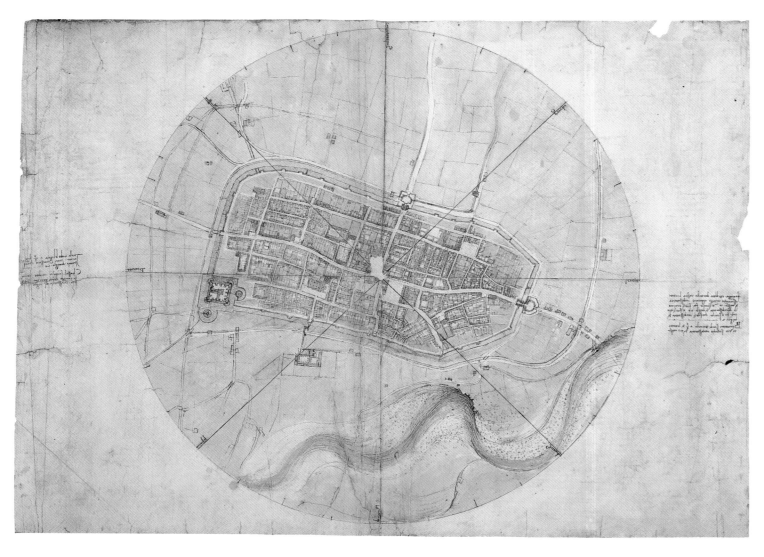

49

Sketches of the streetplan of Imola

1502
Pen and ink
286 x 201 mm (11¼″ x 7¹⁵⁄₁₆″)
No watermark.
RL 12686

50

Imola

1502
Black-chalk underdrawing, pen and ink,
coloured washes, stylus lines
440 x 602 mm (17⁵⁄₁₆″ x 23¹¹⁄₁₆″)
No watermark.
RL 12284

Imola is a town south-east of Bologna on the Via Aemilia, the Roman road running in a straight line along the foot of the Appennines from Rimini to Piacenza. By late 1502 it was the northernmost point of Cesare Borgia's territory, and he lodged there with his forces in the autumn of that year, receiving Niccolò Macchiavelli as the Florentine ambassador for two months. This was probably the only occasion that Leonardo, then in Borgia's retinue, would have had the time or the inclination to produce a map of the detail and sophistication of cat. 50. The sketch-plan, showing the lengths of the streets, and the circular form of the fin-

ished map with stylus lines radiating from the centre demonstrate that Leonardo constructed the map by a combination of measured distances on the ground and measured angles from a fixed point (the tower of the Palazzo Comunale at the central crossroads), a method described by Leon Battista Alberti in his *Ludi mathematici* of 1450.

Cat. 49 was apparently folded into quarters before Leonardo drew on it; this and the lack of a consistent orientation to the writing strongly suggest that the sketches were compiled by Leonardo as he paced out the streets, paper in hand. The distances are recorded in *braccia*, the

usual unit of measurement of the time (one *braccio*, literally an arm, being a little under two modern feet). At the upper left is a plan of the south-east quarter of the town, two sketches of the fortress, and a measured plan of the eastern gate; at the upper right, a plan of the south-western quarter. The northern gate is studied to the lower right, with a plan of the northern half of the town; here Leonardo ran out of space at the edge of the paper, and the increasing confusion as he tried to fit the streets together compelled him to make a fresh start and survey the north-eastern quarter again, in the lower left part of the sheet – slight discrepancies in the street lengths show that he measured the distances a second time.

These perfunctory notes give no hint of the grandeur of the final product, cat. 50, the most accurate and beautiful map of its era. On a scale of close to 1:6000, the town is treated as a pure ground plan, with the columns of churches, cloisters and colonnades shown as tiny circles or dots, and every house with its courtyard and boundary delineated. Leonardo almost entirely eliminated topography from his map, but the result is not coldly scientific: the subtle irregularities in the rectilinear street plan, and the coiling of the river Santerno – Leonardo was incapable of drawing moving water lifelessly – give the town the appearance of an organism seen through a microscope.

The map is divided into eight according to the wind-rose tradition, and Leonardo named the winds around the edge of the circle: *Septantrione, Grecho, levante, Scirocho, Mezzodi, libecco, Ponente, Maesstro*. Each octant is itself divided into eight by stylus lines, giving 64 divisions of about 5½° each, and these subdivisions and winds are used to give the directions

Preceding double page: detail of cat. 50

and distances to other towns, in the margins of the sheet: *Imola sees [vede] Bologna at five-eighths from the west [ponente] towards the north-west [maesstro] at a distance of 20 miles ... Faenza is seen from Imola exactly half way between east [levante] and south-east [sscirocho] at a distance of ten miles ...* and so on. These directions are copied from MS. L, Leonardo's notebook during his time with Borgia, which also contains detailed measurements of the fortifications of Cesena and Urbino. They are virtually useless as they stand, coiling around the small pages of the notebook as Leonardo paced out the distances between the bastions, and it is likely that Leonardo made comparable maps, now lost, of the defences of those towns.

It has been observed in an exhaustive study by Fausto Mancini (1979) that the Imola map shows no buildings erected after 1474 other than the Palazzo Riario and the reconstructed fortress; Mancini inferred that cat. 50 was drawn by a Danesio Maineri in the 1470s, and that Leonardo merely redrew the town walls and annotated the sheet. But Leonardo's authorship of every detail of cat. 50 cannot be questioned on grounds of style; it is much more likely that Leonardo relied on an earlier (and technically cruder) map for his information on the houses and courtyards, and that he incorporated these details into a plan of the city that – as confirmed by cat. 49 – he himself surveyed.

51

Central Italy

ca. 1502
Black-chalk underdrawing, pen and ink, brown and blue washes
317 x 449 mm (12½″ x 17¹¹⁄₁₆″), upper corners torn
No watermark
RL 12277

Leonardo's interest in the habits of rivers attained its fullest expression in this map, showing the western coast of Italy from Civitavecchia, north of Rome, to the Gulf of La Spezia, a distance of some 170 miles, at a scale of 1:570,000; north is to the left. In the south (to the right) are the Tiber and the lakes of Chiana (now drained) and Trasimeno; to the upper left are the cities of Emilia-Romagna as far east as Rimini, in the centre of the upper margin. The Arno is shown in greatest detail, flowing from the centre of the sheet to the coast at lower left. It has been pointed out by Susan Kish that Leonardo's model for the map was a manuscript of *ca.* 1470 then in the library at Urbino, which Leonardo visited in the entourage of Cesare Borgia; this would give a date of 1502 or shortly afterwards, which is supported by the style of the map.

The area covered, the distortions (in particular the random wavy lines that delineate the Po, upper left), and even many of the spellings are taken exactly from the Urbino map; but Leonardo transformed his model by using contour shading, abandoning the 'molehill' convention seen in cats. 52–53. The tones are relative, not absolute – the valley floor of the upper Arno, for instance, is left white although it is much higher than the coastal hills, which are washed dark brown – but the sense of objectively recorded terrain stripped of picturesque detail is unequalled by any map of its time.

The one area where Leonardo has elaborated upon the accuracy of his model is the upper reaches of the Arno and the course of its main tributary, the Sieve, where mere streams, and villages around the southernmost bend of the Arno, are drawn and named. Leonardo presumably based this portion·of the map on personal knowledge, and may have surveyed the area himself, just as – some years later – he was to survey the valleys north of Brescia (RL 12673–74).

The concentration on terrain, rather than towns and roads, and the inscriptions in Leonardo's most crabbed mirror-writing, suggest that cat. 51 was made for his own future reference; but a tracing of the map in the Codex Atlanticus (f. 334r) is labelled only with the villages at the head of the Arno, on the borders with the Romagna, and this tracing may therefore have been made directly in connection with Leonardo's work for Borgia.

The area to the right of centre is studied in greater detail in cat. 52; the Arno valley to lower left is the subject of cats. 53–55.

52

The Val di Chiana

ca. 1502
Black chalk underdrawing, pen and ink,
watercolour and bodycolour
338 x 488 mm (13⁵⁄₁₆″ x 19³⁄₁₆″)
No watermark
RL 12278

The central area of this elaborate map, covering about thirty miles between Arezzo at upper left and Chiusi at centre right, is fairly accurate. Despite the 'mole-hill' convention, which gives the impression of a bird's-eye view, there is no

Detail of cat. 51

foreshortening of distances in the *Val di Chiana*. North is to the left; Siena can be seen at lower centre, and Perugia is to the upper right. But the edges of the sheet are seriously distorted, squashing the Tiber along the upper edge, condensing a broad turn of the Arno into a sharp bend at the left, and introducing the lake of Bolsena, and even the sea, into the lower right corner.

A sheet in the Codex Atlanticus (f. 336r) shows the roads and streams around Castiglione and Montecchio in great detail, with some distances marked in *braccia* that were presumably paced out by Leonardo himself, but it is inconceivable that he surveyed the whole area of

cat. 52 himself. Another sheet at Windsor (fig. 14) shows a bird's-eye view of the central area listing the distances between Castiglione (above the lake of Chiana), Foiano (on the lower shore) and other towns in the vicinity; these distances have been crossed through, perhaps indicating that Leonardo referred to them when constructing cat. 52.

There are the remains of blobs of sealing wax around the edges of the verso, which would have been used to fix the map to a board or wall. Every village and river is named in conventional, and rather formal, left-to-right script, implying that the sheet was made for someone other than Leonardo himself. It has been

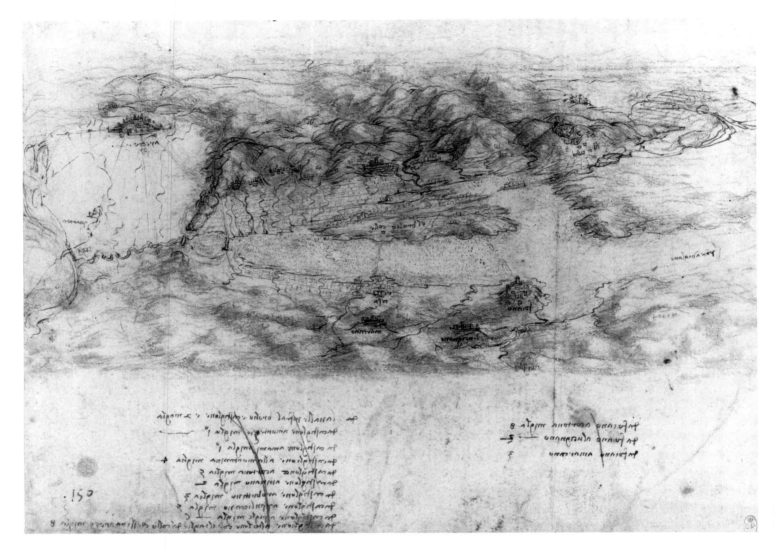

Fig. 14
Leonardo da Vinci
A bird's-eye view of the Val di Chiana
Black-chalk underdrawing, pen and ink, wash,
209 x 281 mm (8¼" x 11¹⁄₁₆")
RL 12682

suggested that the map was related to Leonardo's plans for canalizing the Arno, as a study for the damming of the lake of Chiana to allow a constant flow of water through the Arno during the year. This would be supported by the detail with which the lake of Chiana is drawn, but there is no indication of a hydraulic scheme, which one would expect if the map had been made to demonstrate the feasibility of Leonardo's plans.

Alternatively, both cat. 52 and fig. 14 have been connected with a revolt in Arezzo instigated by one of Cesare Borgia's generals, Vitellozzo Vitelli, in June 1502. This may be too ingenious: Arezzo does not appear to be any more prominent on either map than its size would warrant, and the important roads radiating from the city are misleadingly schematic. But as it is clear that the map was made for somebody other than Leonardo to consult, it may well have been drawn during his time with Borgia in 1502 – though the drawing is of such an unusual type that it is impossible to confirm this date on stylistic grounds.

Detail of cat. 52

53

A bird's-eye map of western Tuscany

ca. 1503–04
Black-chalk underdrawing, pen and ink, wash,
blue bodycolour
275 x 401 mm (10¹³⁄₁₆″ x 15¹³⁄₁₆″)
No watermark
RL 12683

This map of western Tuscany, from
Volterra at lower left to Lucca at upper
right, is not as naïve as it might appear:
although the first impression is of a bird's-
eye view, from some twenty miles above
Florence, the perspective is only apparent,
as in cat. 52. The layout of the towns is
actually correct in the plane of the paper,
and distances may be measured on a scale
of a little over 1:200,000 without having
to account for foreshortening; north is
to the right.

The area shown is that which concerned the Florentines in the siege of Pisa,
which they had been maintaining in a
fairly dilatory manner since the 1490s –
the Pisans could hold out as long as they
maintained their maritime trade. In
1503–04 the Republic tried to bring
matters to a head, and Leonardo was consulted on a plan to divert the waters of the
Arno towards Livorno, thus cutting off
Pisa's access to the sea. As the inscriptions
are left to right and there are traces of
sealing wax on the verso (like cat. 52), the
map was possibly made by Leonardo for
the purposes of demonstration at this
time. The route of the intended diversion
can be seen on cat. 55, and digging began
in August 1504. But the Arno proved
uncooperative (this should have been no
surprise to Leonardo, who usually had the
healthiest respect for the power of water)
and, amid growing unrest about unpaid
wages, the project was abandoned after
two months.

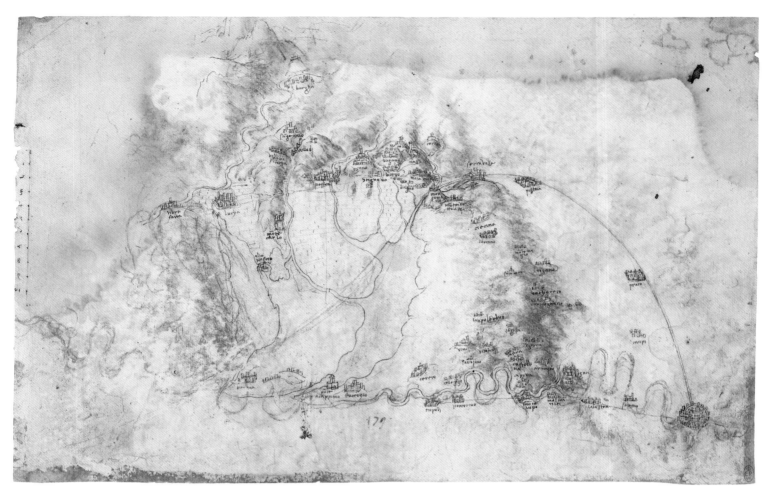

54

The Arno valley with the proposed route of a canal

ca. 1503–04
Black-chalk underdrawing and some pounce-marks, pen and ink, wash; water-stained
240 x 367 mm (9⁷⁄₁₆″ x 14⁷⁄₁₆″)
No watermark
RL 12685

55

The Arno valley with the proposed route of a canal

ca. 1503–04
Black-chalk underdrawing, pen and ink, brush and ink, wash, pricked for transfer
335 x 482 mm (13³⁄₁₆″ x 19″)
No watermark
RL 12279

The Arno is not navigable as far as Florence, mainly because of the rapids in the ravine between Signa and Montelupo, at the southern end of the Monte Albano ten miles west of Florence. The idea of a canal to bypass this stretch of the river – with the consequent commercial and military advantages – was not Leonardo's, and had been suggested at least as early as 1347. The only possible route for such a canal was north from Florence via Prato and Pistoia, somehow through the pass at Serravalle, and into the marshy lake (now drained) north of Fucecchio. From there the detour could either join the Arno at Fucecchio, or could pass via another canal into a lake south of Lucca and thence into the Arno near Vico-pisano.

There were three main difficulties with the scheme, all of which were addressed by Leonardo in his earliest surviving plan (C.A. f. 46r–b), dating from the early 1490s when he was still in Milan. The first was how to deal with the pass at Serravalle, almost a hundred metres high: somewhat unrealistically, Leonardo favoured cutting straight through, rather than constructing troublesome locks. Secondly, the Arno is a mountain torrent, often very low in summer, and liable to flooding during the spring thaw and the autumn rains. He suggested damming the lake of Chiana (see cat. 52) at its two ends, with sluices at Arezzo to feed the Arno when low, though he did not confront the problem of flooding. Thirdly, there would have been the huge expense

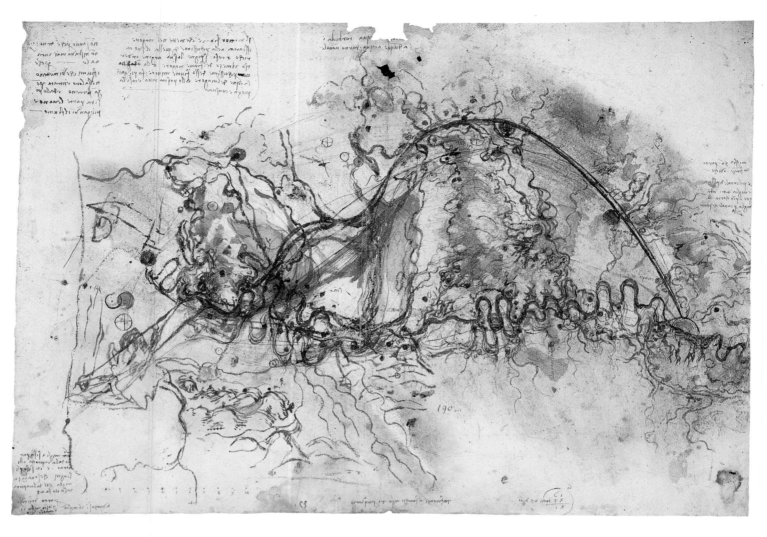

of digging and embanking the canal. Leonardo suggested that the wool merchants' guild, the Arte della Lana, might finance the work, but there is no evidence that his plans were ever detailed enough to consider putting them into practice.

Leonardo's interest in rendering the Arno navigable was revived after his work for Cesare Borgia, and two drawings for the scheme survive at Windsor. Cat. 54 is a map of the area with a scale in miles; the Monte Albano stands at right angles to the Arno, and the line of the canal simply passes in a long, slow curve via Prato and Pistoia, through Serravalle and across the lakes without any consideration being given to the local terrain. Cat. 55 pays more attention to the path of the canal through the lakes – several alternatives are superimposed – but it cuts just as brutally and impractically across the rivers around Prato and Pistoia. It is drawn in unusually loose and vigorous brush and ink, and the sheet is extensively pricked for transfer, suggesting that Leonardo wished to refine the design on another sheet; but the scale of cat. 55 does not correspond with that of cat. 54, where some pounce-marks are visible, nor with that of the most carefully constructed map for the canal, in the Madrid MS. II (ff. 22v–23r), which features a genuine contour line at a height of roughly 80 metres above sea level.

Unlike cat. 54, cat. 55 extends all the way to the coast, but the Arno is not drawn beyond the dark circle that represents Pisa; instead a second detour takes the waters south-west to Livorno. The map may thus also be connected with Leonardo's consultancy work during the siege of Pisa in 1504 (see cat. 53).

56

A stretch of the Arno

1504
Compass holes and stylus lines, black chalk,
pen and ink; water–stained
410 x 257 mm (16⅛″ x 10⅛″)
No watermark
RL 12677

57

A stretch of the Arno

1504
Stylus and hard black chalk underdrawing, pen
and ink, green and blue wash; water–stained
422 x 242 mm (16⅝″ x 9½″)
Watermark: eagle in circle, identical to
Briquet 203
RL 12678

These two maps, on a scale of about
1:9500, show a stretch of the Arno
immediately west of Florence which is
situated above the upper edge of the map;
the Porta al Prato and the Mugnone river
are labelled on cat. 57. Leonardo had
surveyed the river bed in the summer of
1504, and from his preparatory notes
(some of which survive in the Codex
Arundel, ff. 148–49, 271v–272r) he constructed cat. 56, on which numerous
compass holes and stylus lines can be
seen. The outlines were then transferred
by tracing to cat. 57, which was coloured
and annotated by Leonardo in conventional left-to-right script.

Cat. 57 must therefore have been
made for someone else to see, though it
is not entirely clear why. Part of Leonardo's scheme to by-pass the Arno involved the canalization of the river itself
above and below Florence, to allow the
passage of relatively large craft to the
environs of the city, and a companion
drawing to cat. 57 (fig. 15) shows the section of the river to the east of Florence.
Leonardo was aware that a major problem
would be the silting-up of the canal
opposite the mouths of the tributaries,
and both drawings may have been made

cat. 56

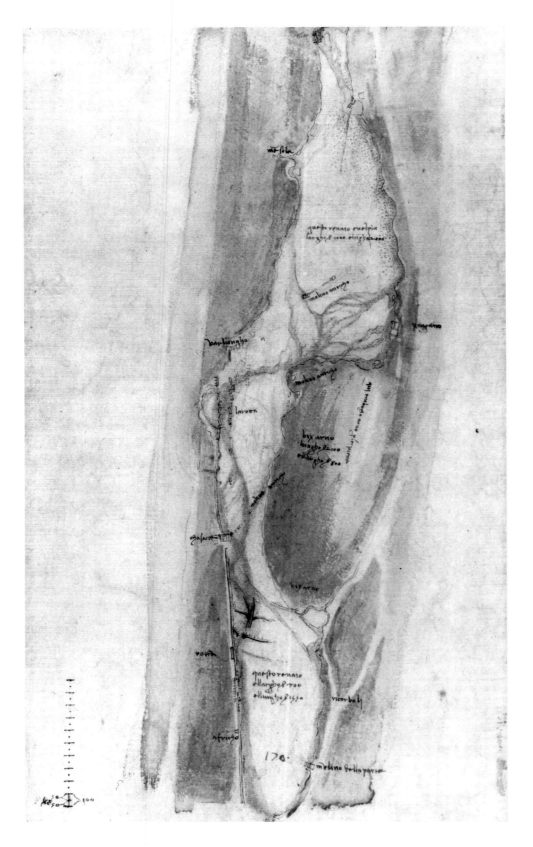

as accurate maps of the areas to be canalized. However, fig. 15 shows several sections where the river bank was crumbling, including one stretch where this was caused by the flow of water through a weir, a problem which he studied in detail on RL 12680. It is thus possible that Leonardo's employment by the Florentine Republic as an engineer during 1504 was not confined to military matters, as in the siege of Pisa in the autumn of that year and at Piombino in November, but also required him to put his mind to such routine subjects as the maintenance of the banks of the Arno, a river given to potentially disastrous flooding.

Fig. 15
Leonardo da Vinci, *A stretch of the Arno*
Stylus and hard black chalk underdrawing, pen and ink, green and blue wash, water-stained, 395 x 222 mm (15⁹/₁₆″ x 8¾″)
RL 12679

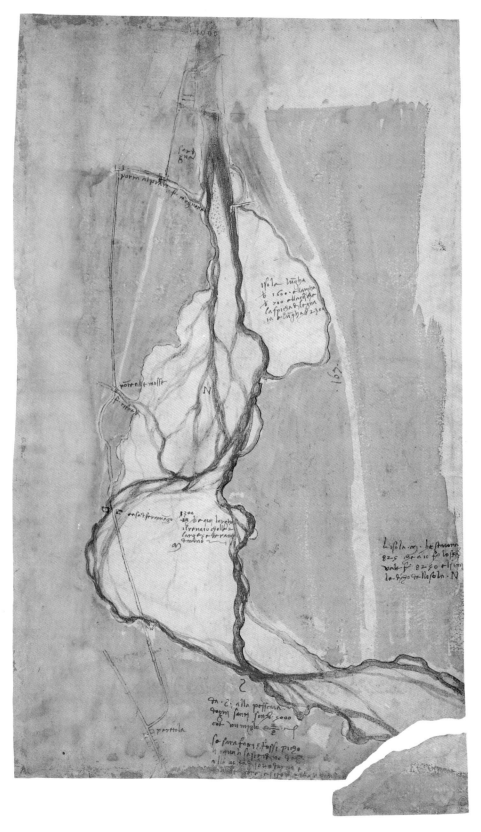

cat. 57

1508–1516
Milan and Rome

After travelling frequently between Milan and Florence for two years, Leonardo finally settled back in Milan around Easter 1508, staying in the area for more than five years. He retained his position as painter and engineer to the King of France, and probably continued to plan a villa for the governor of Milan, Charles d'Amboise; he advised on hydraulic matters, surveyed the valleys north of Bergamo, and in 1510 was consulted on a project for choir stalls in Milan Cathedral.

As an artist, Leonardo finally discharged his responsibilities on the *Virgin*

of the Rocks, and he probably began work on the third and last version of the *St Anne* compositions (cats. 75–80). A proposed equestrian monument to Gian Giacomo Trivulzio, with more than an echo of the fruitless Sforza monument of fifteen years before, would have been the major undertaking of the last decade of Leonardo's life if anything tangible had been carried out (cats. 62–64). Perhaps more important now to Leonardo than artistic projects were his scientific pursuits.

Between 1508 and 1513 Leonardo was preoccupied with research into anatomy and the motion of water (cats. 65–71), subjects which often overlapped. Many of his anatomical drawings were based on his dissection of the centenarian in Florence in the winter of 1507–08 (see cat. 48). Leonardo's analyses of visceral function were primarily in terms of hydrodynamics, for he had no understanding of biochemistry: his many observations on the turbulence of flowing water and understanding of the formation of vortices lay behind his acute analysis of the functioning of the heart's valves.

Leonardo's finest anatomical work was carried out in the winter of 1510–11, when possibly he was working in the university hospital in Pavia alongside Marcantonio della Torre (see cat. 67). This brief period of stability and achievement was to be disrupted in 1511 with the deaths both of his collaborator, Marcantonio, and of his patron, Charles d'Amboise. On Charles's death, Gian Giacomo Trivulzio became joint governor of the city, and the stability of French rule in the area rapidly deteriorated. By December 1511 Swiss forces, supported by both the Pope and the Holy Roman Emperor, were outside Milan.

The Swiss finally took a part of the city in July 1512 and installed as Duke Massimiliano Sforza, son of Ludovico (who had died in 1508). The French managed to hold the Castello until 19 September 1513, and any artistic patronage was stifled by the impossibly volatile political and commercial situation in Milan. Although he retained lodgings in the city, Leonardo spent much of this period at the family villa of Francesco Melzi, his young assistant, at Vaprio d'Adda, fifteen miles east of the city. There Leonardo made a number of charming tiny landscape drawings, planned improvements to the villa, and continued his anatomical work, with oxen and dogs as subjects.

Finally on 24 September 1513 Leonardo and four assistants left Milan. Passing through Florence, where the Medici had recently been restored to power, they were in Rome by 1 December. Rooms were obtained for Leonardo in the Belvedere of the Vatican by Giuliano de' Medici, the brother of Giovanni de' Medici, recently elected Pope Leo X; such immediate favour suggests that Leonardo had been assured of Giuliano's patronage even before he left Milan.

Leonardo's artistic achievements in Rome are hard to define. In a city that during the previous five years had become the centre of the High Renaissance, with Michelangelo's Sistine Chapel frescos newly unveiled and Raphael at work in the Stanze, little that Leonardo accomplished has survived. Vasari writes about a small *Madonna and Child*, already ruined by his day, a portrait of a boy, and an unspecified painting for the Pope; and when Antonio de' Beatis visited Leonardo in France in 1517, he saw a portrait of a "certain Florentine lady, done from the life at the instance of the late Giuliano de' Medici". Leonardo continued his anatomical researches in the hospital of Santo Spirito, but soon he was slandered before the Pope and accused of sacrilegious practices, and much to his vexation he was forbidden to perform dissections.

Two drafts of letters to Giuliano reveal Leonardo's frustrated state of mind at this time, and he must have relished his frequent journeys outside Rome, to Civitavecchia, Parma and Sant'Angelo in 1514, and to Milan (now back under French control) in December 1515. In 1515 Leonardo also spent some time in Florence, recording the measurements of the new Medici stables and planning a palace for Lorenzo di Piero de' Medici, nephew of Giuliano, who that year had been created Governor of Florence; it is possible that the active patronage of Giuliano had lapsed by then, and that Leonardo's move to France the following year was not prompted by the death of Giuliano in March 1516.

The French court had been well aware of Leonardo's talents since the occupation of Milan in 1499, and his virtuosity had been brought to the attention of Francis I (who succeeded Louis XII early in 1515) by the design of a mechanical lion commissioned by the Florentine community in Lyons to welcome the king into that city in July 1515. The strong links between the Medici and the French court had led to the marriage of Giuliano de' Medici to Philiberta of Savoy, aunt of Francis I, and it has also been speculated that Leonardo may have been in the entourage of Leo X when the Pope met the French king in Bologna in December 1515. Our last record of Leonardo's presence in Rome is a set of measurements of the church of San Paolo fuori le mura, dated to August 1516 (C.A. f. 172v–b); whatever the circumstances of Francis's offer of employment to Leonardo, by January 1517 he was in the Loire valley, where he was to spend the remainder of his life.

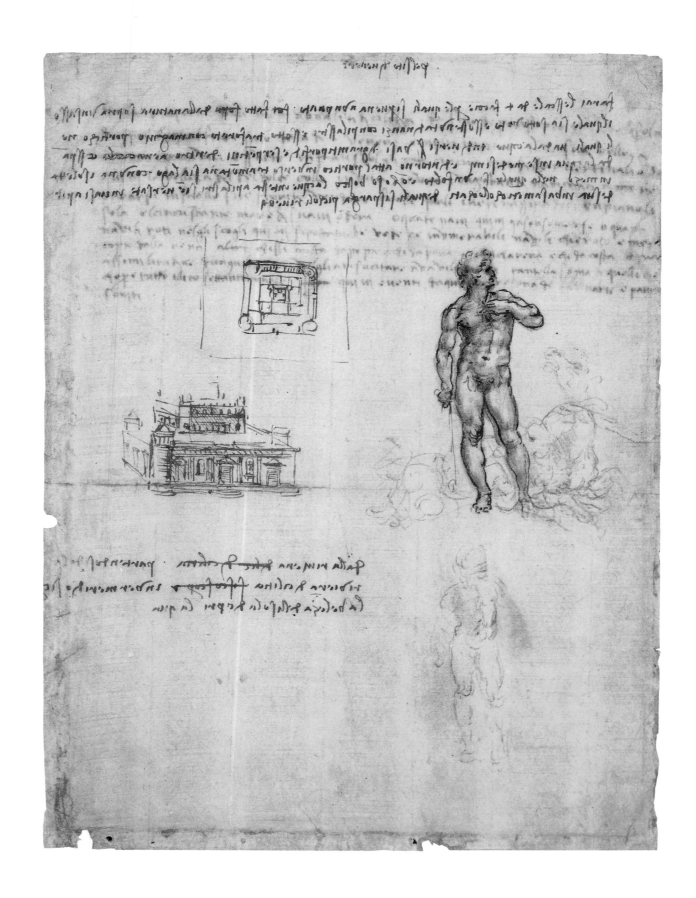

58
Studies for a palace and a figure of Neptune

ca. 1506–09
Black chalk, pen and ink
270 x 201 mm (10⅝" x 7¹⁵⁄₁₆")
No watermark
RL 12591

Leonardo was a member of the committee which met on 25 January 1504 to decide where Michelangelo's marble *David* ought to be placed. The two figure studies on this sheet are derived in pose from the *David*, but Michelangelo's poised youth has become a robust, middle-aged man of Leonardo's post-*Anghiari* type, and the upper figure has been adapted by the inclusion of at least one sea-horse. This relates the sheet to the highly finished drawing of *Neptune* which Leonardo executed for his friend Antonio Segni shortly before the latter left Florence for Rome, probably in 1504.

These two connections would point to a date for the sheet of around 1504, but the architectural studies seem to be related to Leonardo's work for the French occupiers of Milan in the years after 1506, which included a projected villa for Charles d'Amboise, the Governor of Milan (described on C.A. f. 271v–a, *ca.* 1506–08). The square building drawn here obliquely and in plan is a fascinating combination of domestic and military motifs: a rich one-storey façade with niches and pedimented doors and windows, terminated by circular corner towers, with the roof rising to a square central tower and internal light provided by a deep, narrow courtyard. The concept is very similar to that of a building drawn in MS. K³, f. 116r, also of *ca.* 1506–08.

The notes on cat. 58 give instructions for the layout of a shrine of Venus, which leads Leonardo into a poetic description of the realm of the goddess at Cyprus; this may have been prompted by his plans for the villa's garden. *Fountains in diverse places* are mentioned, and it is possible that the figure studies are for a Neptune fountain for that garden. The transformation of the *David* into a Neptune would have involved several changes, some iconographic and some arising from the incompatibility of Leonardo's and Michelangelo's sculptural ideals. The emphasis on outline in Michelangelo's sculpture has been eradicated: the *David* is essentially a single-view sculpture which would not adapt easily to a free-standing fountain, and in the brief chalk sketch below Leonardo breaks the frontality of the pose by pulling the left shoulder backwards, thus twisting the torso and increasing the *contrapposto* of the figure.

59
Three emblems

ca. 1508–09
Traces of black-chalk underdrawing, pen and ink with some wash, blue bodycolour
269 x 195 mm (10⁹⁄₁₆" x 7¹¹⁄₁₆")
No watermark
RL 12701

Each of these carefully drawn emblems has the theme of constancy. The plough has below it the words *hostinato rigore* (obstinate rigour). The second emblem shows the body of a compass turned continuously by a waterwheel, while the needle continues to point at a star; the inscription below, *Destinato rigore*, does not translate easily but is roughly 'determined rigour'. To the left is the motto *nona revolutione chiattale stella effisso*, crudely 'He is not turned around who has such a fixed star'. The third emblem shows a lantern the candle of which is blown from all sides by personifications of winds, but the flame is not disturbed.

The devising of emblems was a standard duty of a court artist, and had been practised by Leonardo since his years at the Sforza court (cat. 28). The three emblems here are studied on other sheets (RL 12282, 12700) that may be dated to 1508 or 1509, when Leonardo was again working in Milan, then occupied by the French; indeed it has been discerned that the star of the second emblem contains three tiny fleurs de lys, the symbol of France.

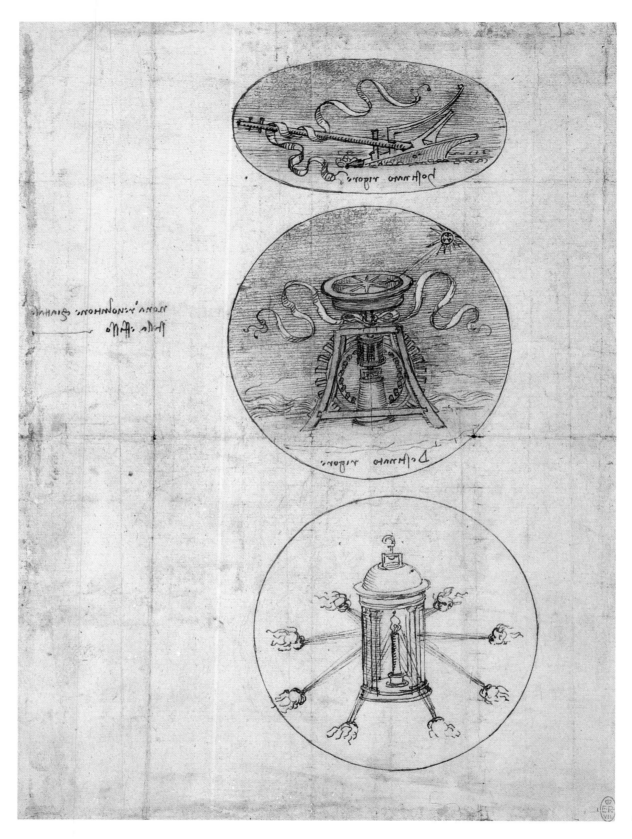

cat. 59

cat. 60

cat. 61

60

Head of a youth in profile

ca. 1510
Red and black chalks on red prepared paper
217 x 153 mm (8⅛″ x 6″)
No watermark
RL 12554

61

Head of a man in profile

ca. 1510
Red and black chalks on red prepared paper
222 x 159 mm (8¾″ x 6¼″)
No watermark
RL 12556

The juxtaposition of youth and maturity, first seen in cat. 5, was a theme of Leonardo's studies of heads throughout his life. These two drawings were not prepared as pendants – the difference in scale militates against this – but they were clearly conceived in the same vein, and at about the same time, as representatives of ideal types.

The differences between the two are not confined to physiognomy and musculature: the manner of drawing also conveys something of the lives of the two subjects. The long, curving horizontal passes that build up the smoothly rounded skin of the youth in cat. 60 suggest a layer of juvenile fat that has not been shed with the passing of adolescence. The barely defined jaw, merging with the slight pouch of a double chin, the straight nose and the untroubled eyes testify to a life of idle luxury. By contrast the battered skin of the ageing man of cat. 61, sagging over the firm muscle, is constructed not of separate strokes but of small areas of chalk, lightly rubbed into the surface, strengthened in places by stumping and by wetting the tip of the chalk, giving wide variations of surface texture that convey a lifetime of trials and ordeals.

Both drawings were worked over by Leonardo in black chalk, not only for emphasis and to adjust some outlines, but also to give an added depth and richness to the hair, which in the youth is drawn with an attention to its decorative qualities that matches the extreme formalism of the *Deluge* drawings (cats. 96–99). Until about 1490 Leonardo's youths usually have shoulder-length hair, straight at the crown and waving towards the ends; after this date most have quite tight curls. This transition coincides with the entry into Leonardo's entourage, at the age of ten, of his troublesome assistant Gian Giacomo Caprotti, known as Salaì, described by Vasari as "having beautiful curly hair, in which Leonardo took great delight"; Lomazzo, in a manuscript in the British Library, wrote explicitly of the homosexual nature of the relationship between Leonardo and Salaì (see Pedretti 1991). While it is not tenable to describe every head of a young man after this date as a portrait of Salaì in the strictest sense, it is surely not fanciful to imagine Leonardo's ideal of youthful beauty being transformed by his first encounter with the boy who was to stay with him for the rest of his life.

The Trivulzio monument

62

A sketch for a monument to Gian Giacomo Trivulzio

ca. 1508
Pen and ink
37 x 28 mm (1⁷⁄₁₆″ x 1⅛″), irregular
No watermark
RL 12353A

63

Sketches for a monument to Gian Giacomo Trivulzio

ca. 1508–10
Pen and ink on coarse paper
278 x 196 mm (10¹⁵⁄₁₆″ x 7¹¹⁄₁₆″), a square patch added at upper centre
No watermark
RL 12353

64

Sketches for a monument to Gian Giacomo Trivulzio

ca. 1508–10
Pen and ink on coarse paper
280 x 198 mm (11″ x 7¹³⁄₁₆″)
No watermark
RL 12355

cat. 62

cat. 63

cat. 64

Gian Giacomo Trivulzio was a mercenary military leader who came to prominence in preparing the French forces for the invasion of Milan in 1499. For this he was appointed a Marshal of France, then Marquis of Vigevano, and, after the death of Charles d'Amboise in 1511, joint Governor of Milan. His will of 22 February 1507 made provision for a chapel and tomb in San Nazaro, Milan, although he did not die until 1518. Our only evidence that this tomb was intended to be an equestrian monument designed by Leonardo is a detailed cost estimate in the Codex Atlanticus (f. 179v–a) entitled *Sepulcro di Messer Giovani Jacomo da Trevulzo*. The building of the chapel was begun in 1511 to designs by Bramantino, but no subsequent document or early biography ties Leonardo to the project, and it is unlikely that he began any tangible work on the monument.

Leonardo's estimate for the monument included separate costings for materials and labour, and these two components are not entirely consistent. Nonetheless we can deduce the general design of the monument from the estimate: a horse and rider, life size, on a decorated marble slab supported by eight columns; beneath the slab, the effigy, on a catafalque resting on six harpies; the whole on a base supported by pedestals, interspersed with figurated panels. The costing accounts for the carving of "eight figures", but as this was to be relatively inexpensive (only a little more each than for the carving of each rosette for the soffit) and the figures were not accounted for as separate blocks of marble, they must have been reliefs, not free-standing statues.

The surviving drawings usually associated with the project are all at Windsor: a few pen-and-ink sketches, and one in red chalk, of the whole monument; a series of more careful drawings, mainly in black chalk, of a horse and rider; and

several detailed studies of the anatomy of the horse. But it is here proposed that of these, only the first group are preparatory for the Trivulzio monument, and that the others date from Leonardo's French period in connection with an unrecorded project. This is discussed on pp. 141–49; here the pen-and-ink sketches alone will be considered.

None of the sketches (cats. 62–64 and fig. 16) shows a design that corresponds fully with the estimate. A sheet devoted to the casting of the horse (RL 12347) includes a small drawing of a walking horse with the rider holding a baton in his outstretched arm, a solution considered in various permutations for both the Sforza monument and the putative French project. This may give the final form of the equestrian group for the Trivulzio monument, but does not include any indication of the architecture.

Cat. 62 is a fragment cut from a sheet in the Codex Atlanticus (f. 83v–b) of *ca.* 1508 that includes some general notes on casting, and is probably the earliest study to survive. The beautifully compact and balanced group, the horse rearing over a fallen foe while the rider rocks back and steadies himself with his sword- or baton-bearing arm, is placed directly on a sarcophagus; there is no effigy. The fallen soldier supports the belly of the horse, not its legs as is more common in such studies, and the grouping is that much more effective for leaving the front half of the horse free, rather than closing the composition in an earthbound circle.

The settings examined in cat. 63 are much more elaborate. That at centre left is strikingly reminiscent of the Tempietto of San Pietro in Montorio, Rome, begun probably in 1502 by Bramante, whom Leonardo had known a decade earlier in

Sforza Milan. The larger study to the right and that at lower centre show a rectangular, pedimented form from front and back; possibly the central study is a side view of the same design, but the details are too vague to confirm this. Figures crouching on the entablature are presumably captives symbolic of Trivulzio's military triumphs. It is often assumed that Leonardo took this motif from Michelangelo's first design for the tomb of Julius II, of 1505, but it is unclear to what extent Michelangelo's design was known to other artists. The motif was of course a standard feature of antique Victory representations, and here the captives echo an earlier drawing by Leonardo for the tiburio of Milan Cathedral (C.A. f. 148r–a, *ca.* 1487–88).

The architecture of the two lower studies on cat. 64 approaches the clarity of the final design as far as it can be reconstructed from the estimate, although the horse is still shown rearing. The captives are shackled to free-standing columns around the base of the monument, and the small sketch at lower left, the last to be drawn on this sheet, shows how Leonardo's thoughts kept returning to a more grandiose setting for his horse, reminiscent of a triumphal arch.

The architecture of fig. 16 is a development of the lower right sketch of cat. 64; the sarcophagus is more resolved, and on it an effigy can be seen for the first time. The horse is now walking, and the red-chalk element, with the horse in profile, is close to the small drawing on the sheet of casting studies (RL 12347). Although the captives are still free-standing figures, the architecture corresponds in many other respects with the estimate. This is our last glimpse of Leonardo's development of the Trivulzio monument, and it was to be the basis of his return to an equestrian project some ten years later (cats. 81–87).

Water studies

65

Studies of flowing water

ca. 1509–11
Red chalk, pen and ink
205 x 203 mm (8¹⁄₁₆″ x 8″)
Watermark: eight-petalled flower (cut), not in Briquet
RL 12661

66

Studies of flowing water

ca. 1509–11
Red chalk, pen and ink
290 x 202 mm (11⁷⁄₁₆″ x 7¹⁵⁄₁₆″)
No watermark
RL 12660

Water obsessed Leonardo throughout his life. His earliest dated drawing (Uffizi, P. 253), of 1473, is a landscape showing a river cascading over rocks and streaming away down a valley; his final sheets, forty-five years later, are haunted by visions of deluges destroying the earth. Leonardo's scientific study of the behaviour of water began as an offshoot of his work towards a treatise on painting around 1490, but in the years around 1508–11 he pursued hydraulics as a subject in itself. At this time his study of the internal organs of man was also at its peak, and as he was oblivious to biochemistry (other than the medieval traditions of the humours), many of his explanations of the body's functions are in terms of hydrodynamics.

There are hundreds of observations on the movement of water throughout Leonardo's notes at this time, and although certain themes recur – in particular his astute analyses of complex motions in terms of linear and circular components – the superabundance of particular cases prevented him from ever realising a set of generally applicable laws.

Cat. 65 studies the fall of a stream of water into a pool and the patterns of the resulting bubbles, drawn as chrysanthemum-like eddies. The notes attempt, tortuously, to analyse the behaviour of these bubbles. The main drawings of cat. 66 investigate the flow of torrential water past a board (*asse*) held at various angles; Leonardo must have been struck by the fact that the patterns were stable and repeatable, evidence that the flow was not random and chaotic but subject to universal laws. In the surrounding notes he struggles to frame such principles in terms of incidence, percussion and reflection, the same language he had used for the behaviour of light and of solids: ... *if the wave is at an angle to the normal course of the water then its reflection will be composite, in the sense that the percussed water, in addition to making a reflected motion along the same obliquity of the incident longitudinal motion, acquires a circular motion.*

The small sketch of the course of a river to the lower right of cat. 66 is an example of the effects of percussion and reflection in practice: a n, *channel, is created by the composite reflection of the flooding of the rivers, which after the said floods remain hollowed out.*

The island is labelled *arosa* – the town Arosa in the Alps, ninety miles north of Milan. Leonardo had surveyed the region to the north of Bergamo (RL 12673–74) probably during the French occupation of that territory in 1509, and presumably had the opportunity to travel as far as Arosa. The combination of red chalk and pen, comparable to the embryological studies (cat. 71), would support a date for cats. 65 and 66 of shortly after those excursions.

cat.

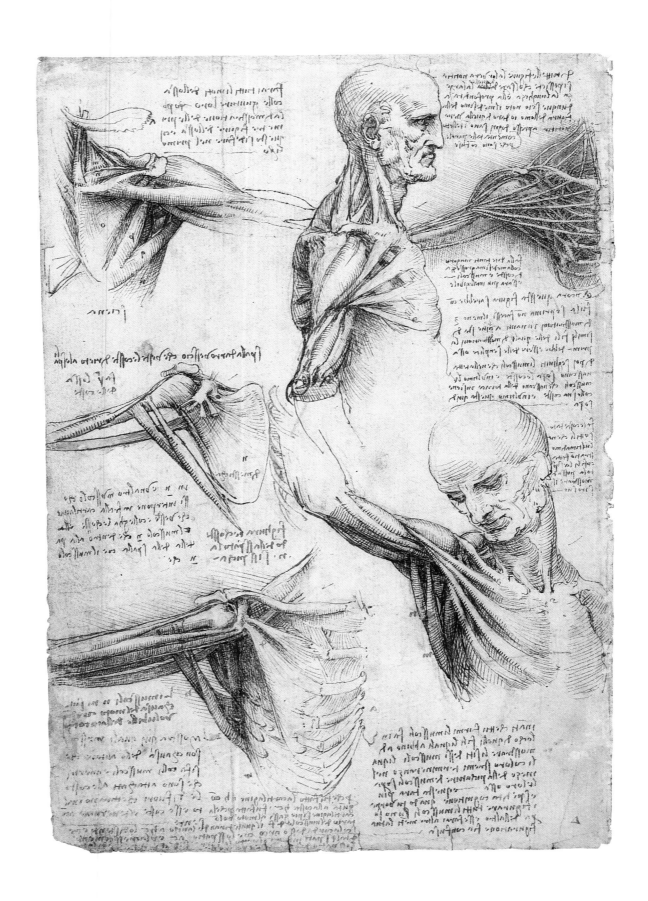

67
The anatomy of the right shoulder

ca. 1510–11
Black-chalk underdrawing, pen and ink,
touches of wash
291 x 203 mm (11⁷⁄₁₆″ x 8″)
Watermark: bow and arrow (cut), not in
Briquet
RL 19003v

The series of osteological and myological drawings from the so called Anatomical MS. A (RL 19000–17) are among Leonardo's finest achievements in the study of human anatomy; one of the sheets is inscribed "this winter of 1510 I believe I will finish all this anatomy", suggesting a date of 1510–11 for the series.

Leonardo's anatomical notes of the period are replete with the notion that every part has a function in a body perfectly made by the Creator – the teleological philosophy of Galen, the great Greek physician of the 2nd century AD. Vasari (1568) stated that Leonardo had collaborated with Marcantonio della Torre, the young professor of anatomy at Pavia, twenty miles south of Milan. Marcantonio was one of a handful of anatomists in northern Italy responsible for the revival of interest in Galen's writings around 1500, which culminated in Vesalius's ground-breaking work forty years later. An acquaintance with Leonardo around 1510 (Marcantonio died in 1511) is the most plausible explanation for the sudden shift towards Galenism in the artist's later investigations.

There is also the question of Leonardo's supply of dissection material – the number of human dissections claimed by him increases from "more than ten" around 1509, to "more than thirty" towards the end of his life. Paolo Giovio recorded in his brief biography of Leonardo (1527) that "he dissected in medical schools the corpses of criminals", and it is possible that Leonardo was actually working alongside Marcantonio in the medical school at Pavia when he compiled Anatomical MS. A in the winter of 1510–11. A note dated 5 January 1511, in Paris MS. G, f. 1v, implies recent contact with the Pavian sculptor Benedetto Briosco, and thus perhaps a stay in Pavia.

In the first drawing of cat. 67, at upper centre, Leonardo has fenestrated pectoralis major to show pectoralis minor running up beneath it to the coracoid process. In fact Leonardo often drew pectoralis major as four separated muscles at this time, suggesting that he had witnessed this normal variation in one of his dissection subjects.

To the right of this is one of Leonardo's most ambitious 'thread diagrams', an attempt to depict a complete system in one drawing by reducing the muscles to single cords along their central lines of force. The paragraph below (which, like many of the notes surrounding Leonardo's drawings in Anatomical MS. A, is about methods of representation rather than immediately about the anatomy) details how Leonardo wished to refine his diagram so that even the scapula was visible in a frontal view: *Furthermore this figure would be confused if you did not make at least three demonstrations before this with similar threads. The first of these demonstrations should be of the simple bones; then follow with the muscles which arise in the breast on the ribs, and finally the muscles which arise from the chest with its assembled ribs; and lastly this* [figure] *here, above. Make the ribs so thin that in the final demonstration made with threads the scapula can be demonstrated in position.*

At upper left is a posterior view of the shoulder with the trapezius, *a*, detached to show its point of insertion. Below this we have an anterior view of the deep muscles with pectoralis minor and coracobrachialis cut away to show subscapularis, *n*, which separates the scapula from the ribs.

Both the lower diagrams show prominently the muscles teres major (*n*) and latissimus dorsi (*m*), and Leonardo notes their responsibility for the rotation of the humerus. Finally, to the left he states that in the act of breathing, pectoralis minor (*d f*) pulls the angle of the ribs upwards, thus expanding the chest cavity.

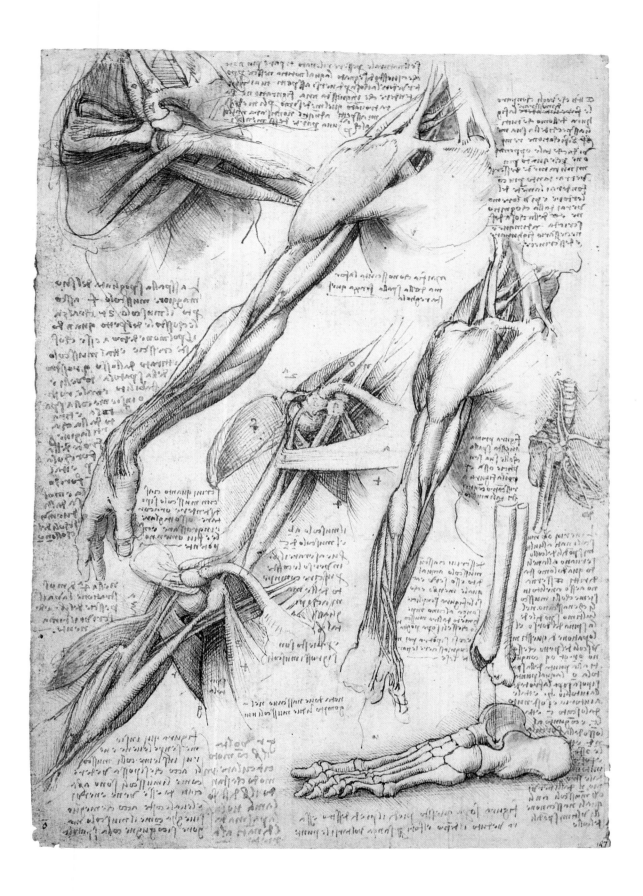

68

The anatomy of the arm, shoulder and foot

ca. 1510–11
Black chalk underdrawing, pen and ink, wash
289 x 201 mm (11⅜″ x 7¹⁵⁄₁₆″)
No watermark
RL 19013v

The first and largest diagram on this beautiful and powerful sheet gives an anterior view of the superficial muscles of shoulder and arm. In this and subsequent drawings trapezius is shown divided with three separate insertions, on the clavicle (*n*), acromion (*o*), and spine of the scapula. The diagram at the centre of the page shows the deltoid lifted away to reveal pectoralis major (*a b*) and latissimus dorsi (*d c*), which Leonardo explains, *serve to press the arm towards the ribs with the result that impetus in the hands is taken from the arm; and for this reason these are such large muscles.*

Elsewhere (RL 19011v) Leonardo identified the analogous muscles in birds as responsible for flight: "It is the same in birds; therefore they are so powerful because all the muscles which lower the wings arise in the chest; these have in themselves greater weight than all the rest of the bird."

A posterolateral view of the same stage of dissection is drawn at the upper left, showing in particular teres major and minor, either side of the long head of triceps, and their insertion on the humerus.

At lower left, labelled by Leonardo as the third stage of the demonstration, Leonardo removes pectoralis major to show fully pectoralis minor (*s t*) and latissimus dorsi (*g r*), and the two heads of biceps. A note states that in the fourth "demonstration" the biceps should be removed, but this drawing is not to be found. Instead we have a study of the bones of the ankle and foot, and,

squeezed into the right margin, a small thread diagram and accompanying note giving an elaborate account of the accessory muscles of respiration.

Throughout the drawings on this page the tip of the acromion is shown as a separate bone, the *summus humerus* of medieval anatomists. It seems improbable that Leonardo should have simply followed tradition in retaining this ossicle whilst relying so completely on observation in the other structures drawn on this page, and it may be that he did see an ununited epiphysis in the subject of a dissection.

69

The anatomy of the throat and of the leg

ca. 1510–11
Black-chalk underdrawing, pen and ink, some wash
290 x 197 mm (11⁷⁄₁₆″ x 7¾″)
No watermark
RL 19002

In several of the sheets in Anatomical MS. A Leonardo started with a note prescribing a working method or an area of the body to be studied, and then proceeded to fill the page with unrelated material; here he began, *put in all the passages which the veins make in the flesh and in their ramifications between the flesh and the skin.* Instead he drew the superficial anatomy of the leg, without comment, and surrounded this with the bulk of his surviving observations on the throat.

The three diagrams along the right margin study the hyoid bone and its relationship to the epiglottis and trachea, the second one showing the epiglottis bent back as a lump of food passes into the oesophagus. At the centre of the sheet are two lateral views of the larynx. The two small drawings and accompanying notes at lower right describe the laryngeal

ventricles, and at lower centre Leonardo depicts the vocal chords viewed from above and in section. He took the view that the voice was produced by turbulence in the flow of air through the rima glottidis; shortly afterwards he would observe a similar structure in the valves and sinuses of the heart, deducing that eddies in the sinuses were responsible for the closing of the valves (see cat. 71).

All these studies are united in the two large drawings to the left of the sheet. Overlapping the upper drawing is a view of the uvula, oropharyngeal isthmus and thyroid eminence; traditional physiology held that phlegm was secreted in the brain, passing through the infundibulum to the pituitary gland. An excess would reach the nose through the cribriform plate of the ethmoid, and thence it would drip from the uvula into the larynx to lubricate the throat and lungs (though Leonardo rejected this, believing instead that the phlegm dripped down the oesophagus to reach the stomach). The very small thyroid gland below the cricoid cartilage suggests that the subject was a dog or a pig, both of which were commonly used for dissection at the time.

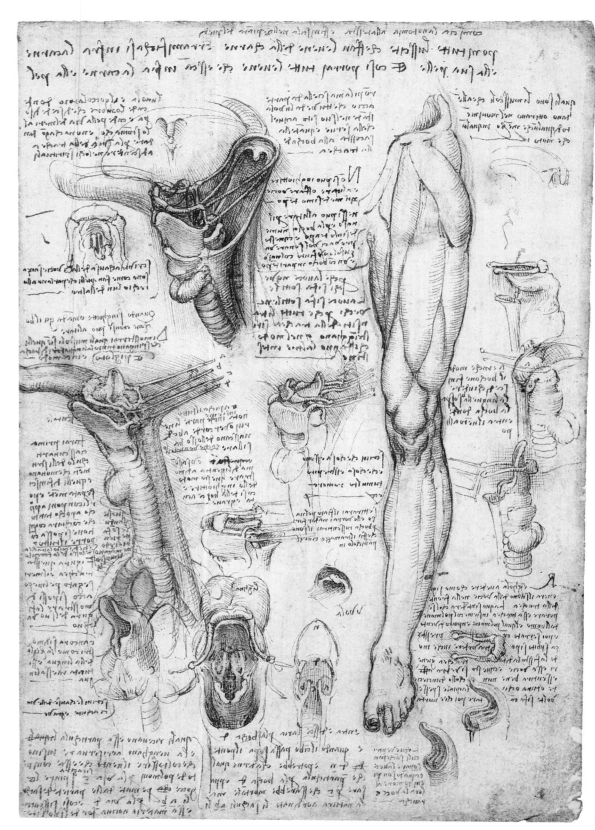

cat. 69

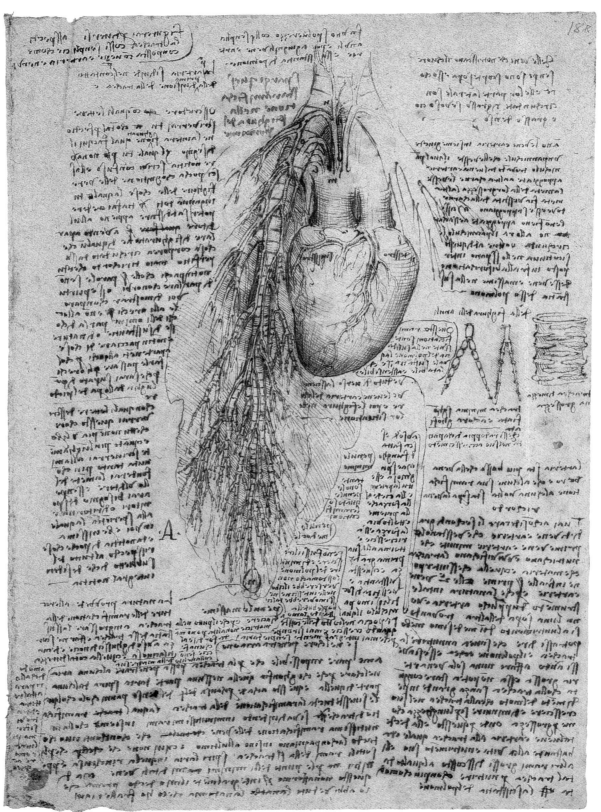

cat. 70

70

The heart and lungs of the ox

ca. 1512–13
Black-chalk underdrawing, pen and ink, on
rough blue paper
286 x 203 mm (11¼″ x 8″)
No watermark
RL 19071

Leonardo's studies of the heart constituted
the most sustained and brilliant of all his
anatomical investigations. He coupled his
knowledge of mechanics and fluid dynamics with his remarkable manual and
observational skills to arrive at an understanding of the structure and operation of
the valves that is in some aspects on a par
with modern research. He identified the
auricles, and described the movements
of diastole and systole: Leonardo was on
the road to discovering the circulation of
the blood, a century before Harvey. Only
a reluctance to abandon the medieval
physiology of the cardiovascular system –
which treated the venous and arterial
trees as independent, the former distrib-
uting 'natural spirit' (nutrition), the latter 'vital spirit' (a life force) – prevented
him from making a last leap of the imagination and realising that the blood flowing out through the arteries returned
through the veins, and that the systems
were connected at the extremes of their
ramifications by invisibly small capillaries.

The heart series is drawn on blue paper
with a thick pen, and is usually, as here,
based on dissection of the ox. One of the
sheets (RL 19077) is inscribed with the
date 9 January 1513, and the others were
probably executed a few months either
side of that date. Only now, towards the
end of Leonardo's anatomical career, does
the text begin to vie with the illustrations
for primacy – several sheets contain solid
blocks of notes with only marginal
sketches; and the relationship between
word and image has changed, drawing
illustrating text and text explaining draw-

ing with an intimacy not found in the
patchworks of cats. 67–69.

Here Leonardo presents a posterior
view of the heart, trachea and bronchial
tree, showing the great and lesser cardiac
veins and the inferior intraventricular and
circumflex branches of the right coronary
artery on the surface of the heart. Most of
the notes are concerned with the venous
and arterial supply of the bronchial tree;
Leonardo also discusses whether or not air
penetrates directly into the pulmonary
system: *To me it seems impossible that air can
penetrate into the heart through the trachea
because if one inflates it, no part of the air
escapes from any part of it, and this occurs
because of the dense membrane with which the
entire ramification of the trachea is clothed.
This ramification of the trachea as it goes on
divides into the most minute branches, together
with the most minute ramification of the vessels, which accompany them in continuous contact right to the end.*

71

The embryo in utero

ca. 1511–13
Black and red chalk underdrawing, pen and
ink, some wash
305 x 220 mm (12″ x 8¹¹⁄₁₆″), left and lower
sides tattered
No watermark
RL 19101

Much of the material for Leonardo's
embryological researches was derived
from animal dissection. But there is evidence that he dissected at least one mis-
carried human embryo, for on the verso
of this sheet and elsewhere he made reasonably accurate drawings of the relative
sizes of the internal organs of an embryo
at four months; and on a few sheets datable to around 1515 are sketches of very
early mammalian embryos, possibly
human at four to six weeks after conception.

The first drawing here, of the female
external genitalia at upper centre, empha-
sizes the adductor muscles of the inner
thigh. This is followed to the right by a
much less accurate (because traditional)
diagram of the muscles of the abdominal
wall, showing slender oblique muscles
attached to the pubis and thus opposing
the pull of the adductor muscles of the
leg. The accompanying notes discuss the
relative sizes of the reproductive organs of
a woman and a cow; Leonardo had dissected a gravid cow around 1508–09, producing a beautiful and accurate drawing
of a foetal calf *in utero* (RL 19055).

The four central drawings, making
striking use of red-chalk underdrawing
for the infant, aim to show that the left
heel of the embryo presses into the per-
ineum, preventing the passage of urine
out of the bladder through the penis –
Leonardo believed that a separate channel
from the bladder to the umbilical cord
allowed the embryo to urinate. He also
considers the question of foetal respiration: *The foetus does not breathe in the body
of the mother because it lies in water, and he
who breathes in water is immediately drowned.*

*Whether the foetus in the body of the
mother can weep or produce any kind of voice
or not. The answer is no, because it does not
breathe nor is there any kind of respiration, and
where there is no respiration there is no voice.*

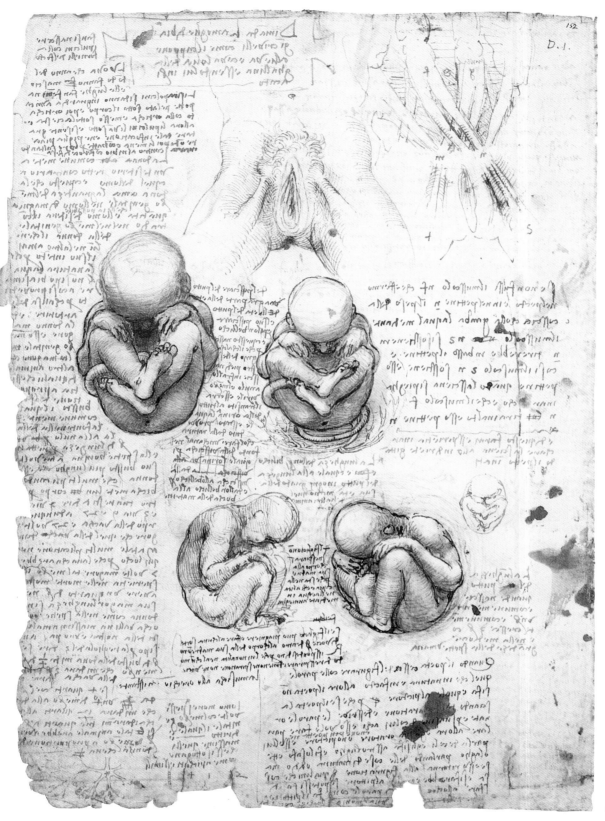

D. 1.

cat. 71

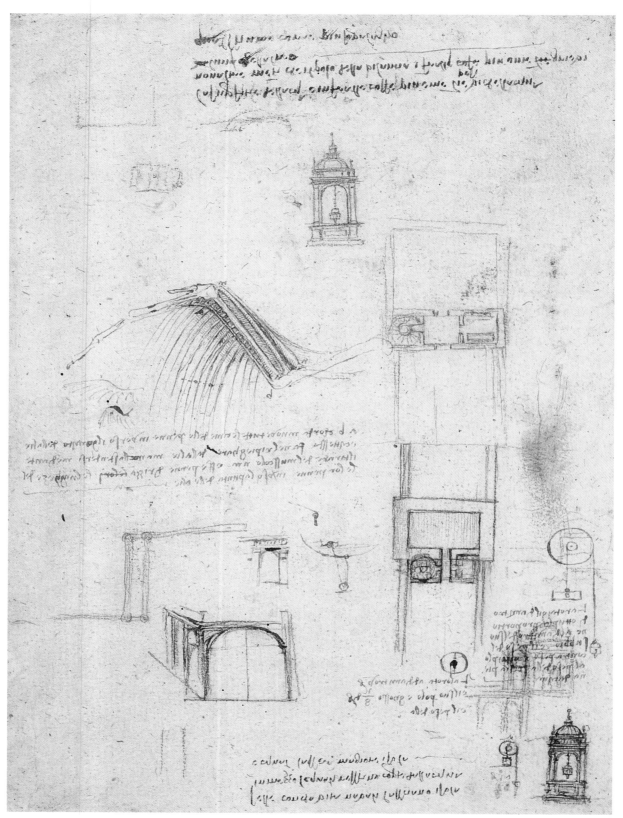

cat. 72

72

Studies of architecture, and of the bones of a bird's wing

ca. 1513
Red chalk, pen and ink; some black chalk
towards the top of the sheet
275 x 201 mm (10¹³⁄₁₆″ x 7¹⁵⁄₁₆″)
No watermark
RL 19107v

The architectural studies on this sheet are connected with a plan to enlarge the Villa Melzi at Vaprio d'Adda, the family seat of Leonardo's assistant Francesco Melzi. A sheet bearing further studies for the same project (RL 19077v) was dated by Leonardo 13 January 1513; Leonardo was living in the villa during 1513, so we cannot be sure whether an enlargement was really in prospect, or was simply an agreeable way for Leonardo to pass his days as a guest of the family. The present sheet gives little idea of the architectural details of the main building, other than a partial sketch of a façade at lower right, obscured with notes in pen and ink.

The two dainty studies of a well-head, presumably for the garden of the villa, led Leonardo to consider a geared axle with a counterweight for drawing the bucket from the well. Leonardo had earlier proposed a wheel with an eccentrically attached cord as a means of converting circular to linear motion in his designs for a mechanical flying machine (Madrid MS. I, ff. 90–91); here the same thoughts led him again to analyse a bird's wing, anatomically at upper left, and reduced to its components – a set of levers arranged in a parallelogram – at centre left: *The tendon a b moves all the tips of the feathers towards the elbow of the wings; and it does this in flexing the wings; but in extending it* [the wing] *by means of the pull of the muscle* n m, *these feathers direct their lengths towards the point of the wings.*

73

The anatomy of the neck

ca. 1515
Pen and ink on rough blue paper
277 x 210 mm (10⅞″ x 8¼″), left and upper left sides tattered
No watermark
RL 19075v

This is probably one of the latest of Leonardo's anatomical drawings. The paper is very rough and appears not to have been sized; Leonardo was thus constrained to use a broad nib, and much of the ink has soaked through to the other side of the sheet.

The note at the top of the sheet reads: *You will first make the spine of the neck with its tendons like the mast of a ship with its side-rigging … Then make the head with its tendons which give it its movement on the fulcrum.*

The main drawing is surprisingly crude, given Leonardo's researches of just a couple of years earlier. Here there are eleven, undifferentiated, cervical vertebrae (rather than the correct seven), the shoulder joint is malformed, and the shoulders are too narrow in relation to the size of the skull. It is apparent that he was not working directly from human material, and was not even particularly concerned with making an anatomically accurate drawing; his aim was to illustrate with a thread diagram a principle he had studied around 1510–11, that a series of antagonistic muscles are responsible for ensuring that the vertebrae are not displaced and for balancing the head on top of the 'fulcrum' of the neck.

74

The Pontine marshes

ca. 1515
Stylus and black-chalk underdrawing, pen and ink, wash, blue bodycolour, touches of red wash
277 x 400 mm (10⅞″ x 15¾″)
No watermark
RL 12684

This is the only elaborate map executed by Leonardo after 1504 to survive. It covers about thirty miles of the coast south of Rome, concentrating on the malarial marshes north of Terracina; the coastline is simplified and exaggerated in its broad curves, and there is an excessively abrupt transition from the flat marshes to the rather uniform hills. Although the drawing is undoubtedly by Leonardo, the inscriptions are in the hand of his pupil, Francesco Melzi.

On 9 January 1515, Giuliano de' Medici, Leonardo's main patron in Rome, obtained the Pontine marshes from his brother, Pope Leo X, and entrusted Domenico de Juvenibus with the planning of a drainage scheme. Several owners of the adjoining lands soon became involved in the project, and on 19 May 1515 a contract was drawn up with Fra Giovanni Scotti da Como to carry out the work, which was successfully completed before 1521 to a design very close to that found in the present map. Although Leonardo is not mentioned in any document, it is hard to avoid the conclusion that he was involved in the planning, for the highly finished nature of the drawing would suggest that it was intended to be seen by a patron.

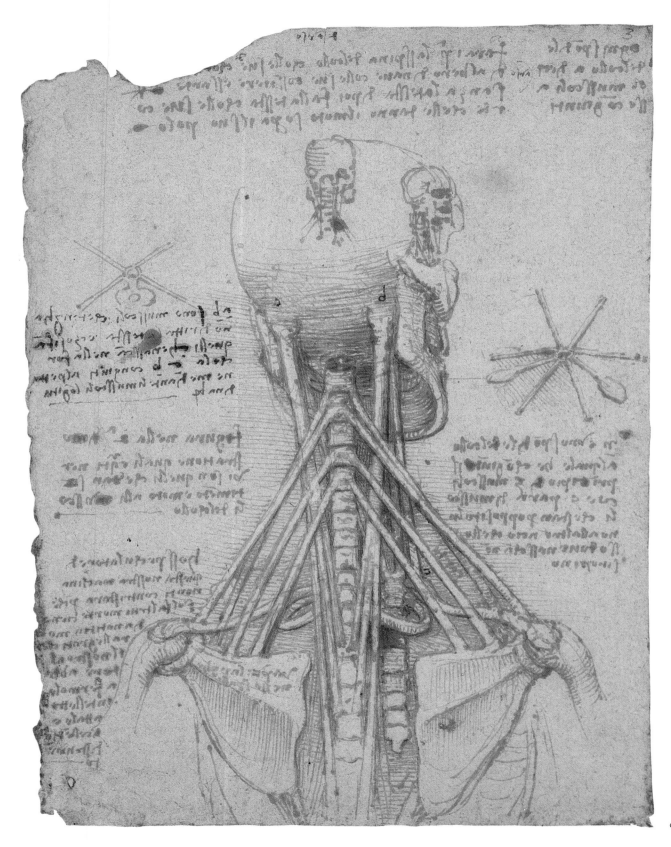

cat. 73

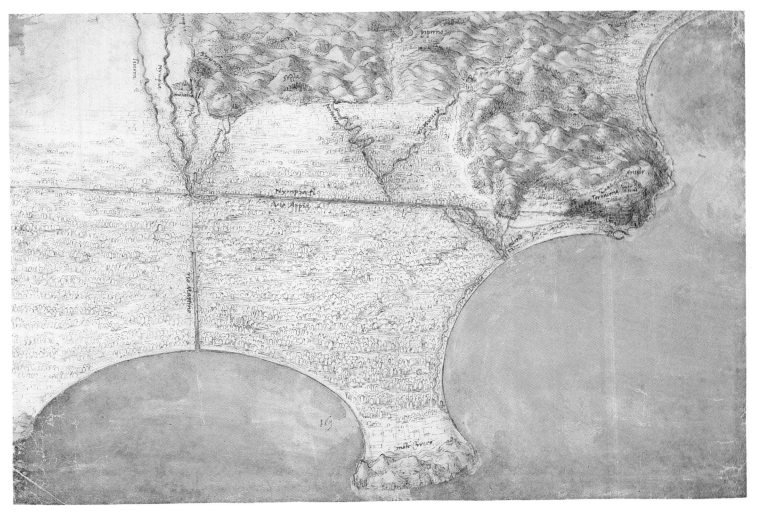

cat. 74

Fig. 17
Leonardo da Vinci
The Madonna and Child with St Anne and a lamb
Oil on panel, 168 x 130 cm (66″ x 51″)
Paris, Musée du Louvre

The Madonna and Child with St Anne and a lamb

75

A study of a boy's torso

ca. 1510
Red chalk, traces of white chalk, on red prepared paper
120 x 143 mm (4¾″ x 5⅝″)
No watermark
RL 12538

76

The head of St Anne

ca. 1510–15
Black chalk
188 x 130 mm (7⅜″ x 5⅛″)
No watermark
RL 12533

77

A rocky outcrop

ca. 1510–15
Black chalk
164 x 201 mm (6⁷⁄₁₆″ x 7¹⁵⁄₁₆″), irregular
Watermark: mermaid in circle, close to Briquet 13885, 13891
RL 12397

78

The drapery of the Madonna's thigh

ca. 1515–17
Charcoal underdrawing, black chalk washed over in places, touches of brown wash, white heightening
164 x 145 mm (6⁷⁄₁₆″ x 5¹¹⁄₁₆″)
No watermark
RL 12530

79

The drapery of St Anne's legs

ca. 1517–18
Black chalk, traces of white chalk, on paper washed buff,
167 x 147 mm (6⁹⁄₁₆″ x 5¹³⁄₁₆″)
Watermark: unicorn, close to Briquet 10405–06
RL 12527

80

The drapery of St Anne's legs

ca. 1517–18
Black chalk, white heightening, on dark grey prepared paper
175 x 140 mm (6⅞″ x 5½″)
No watermark
RL 12526

The subject of the Madonna and Child with St Anne and either a lamb or the infant Baptist, perhaps stemming from a commission from Louis XII after the French occupation of Milan in 1499, occupied Leonardo intermittently for the last two decades of his life. He produced three separate full-size compositions, of which a cartoon (National Gallery, London) and a painting (Louvre) survive in the original; the composition of another cartoon, described in detail in a letter of 3 April 1501 from Fra Pietro da Novellara to Isabella d'Este, is known to us through a copy by Brescianino (formerly Berlin, Kaiser-Friedrichs-Museum).

The painting in the Louvre shows the *Madonna and Child with St Anne and a lamb* (fig. 17) and is the final manifestation of Leonardo's work on the project. The only reference to the panel during Leonardo's lifetime is an account of a visit by Cardinal Luigi d'Aragona to the artist's studio at Amboise on 10 October 1517. His secretary Antonio de' Beatis described the panel as *perfettissimo*, but this was an expression of quality rather than level of finish, for the foreground landscape and the drapery of St Anne were never completed.

Twelve autograph studies of details for the Louvre panel survive, and several black-chalk landscape studies at Windsor, including cat. 77, are probably preparatory for the misty landscape. But no studies of isolated details exist for the two earlier cartoons, which were not committed to panel by Leonardo; there is a sig-

nificant degree of improvisation in the National Gallery cartoon, and it may be that Leonardo executed that cartoon directly from a heavily worked, and apparently final, compositional study now in the British Museum (P. 175), without any intervening studies of details. If the same procedure was followed for the cartoon which presumably preceded the Louvre panel, then it is reasonable to assume that the studies of details were executed after the cartoon, as work on the panel progressed. The drawings would then give some indication of the history of the panel's execution.

These drawings are not all of the same date. Apparently the earliest are three studies for the Child: cat. 75, and two other sheets in the Accademia, Venice, all in a red-on-red technique. The style is very close to that of sheets such as cat. 61, of *ca.* 1510, and this date may be supported by the notes on perspective on the verso of one of the Venice sheets (P. 185), comparable in content to some of the earlier sheets of MS. G (*e.g.* f. 29v) which are securely of around 1510.

There follow a number of black-chalk studies, which are hard to date by style alone. They are characterized by areas of soft chalk brought into focus with a network of sharp lines, and in the absence of a full understanding of the development of Leonardo's chalk style during his later Milanese and Roman years, we can probably do no better than to place them roughly between 1510 and 1515. Cat. 76 is a study for the head of St Anne, seemingly from the life but with the rather rubbery modelling of the flesh that characterizes Leonardo's later drawings. Here the features are small, whereas in the painting the eyes, nose and mouth were enlarged to what later generations came to perceive as the regular, Leonardesque ideal.

Cat. 77 is one of a number of land-

scape studies which may be related to the *St Anne*. It is the closest of the group to the panel, for a similar formation of rocks, with a waterfall cascading towards the left, may be discerned in the area immediately to the left of St Anne's head. But Leonardo changed the scale of the topography in the painting; the tree at the left of the drawing would have been impossibly large if placed with the same proportions in the distant landscape.

The later drawings for the panel are characterized by a range of innovative techniques. A small study of the drapery over the Madonna's legs (RL 12531) is in black chalk alone on red prepared paper, a combination used surprisingly rarely by Leonardo. This study was developed in two exquisite drawings, cat. 78 and a larger sheet in the Louvre (P. 188), of a complexity which reveals the painstaking, even obsessive care with which Leonardo prepared his paintings. A rough outline drawing in charcoal was worked up in closely hatched black chalk, which was gone over with a damp brush to make the modelling smoother still. Touches of brown wash provide colour and give greater depth to the shadows; finally the light on the satiny surface was rendered with a veil of white heightening, applied with the delicacy of a miniaturist. A similar technique was used, on red prepared paper, for a study of the sleeve of the Madonna (RL 12532); and a drawing for the head of the Madonna in the Metropolitan Museum, New York, is in black and coloured chalks – I have not studied this sheet (which is comparatively neglected in studies on Leonardo) in the original, but it appears from photographs to be largely autograph and, if so, is an important example of his experiments in a medium that would be much used by later draftsmen.

The variety of these experimental techniques makes it hard to date the

cat. 75

drawings on stylistic grounds alone, though the area of black chalk around the hips in cat. 78 has the smokiness of late drawings such as the so called *Pointing lady* (RL 12581), suggesting a date towards the end of Leonardo's Roman years, or even into his French period.

Finally there are two sketches of the drapery around the legs of St Anne, combining rubbed areas with very sharp accents of black chalk. Cat. 79 is on paper washed buff which bears a watermark exclusively French in its distribution (see pp. 140–41); cat. 80 is drawn on dark-grey prepared paper and heightened with white – this technique was also used by a member of Leonardo's studio for four copies of details of the composition (RL

12528, 12535–37), two of which also bear French watermarks. Thus material evidence supports the stylistic impression that cats. 79 and 80 were executed by Leonardo in France, after 1516.

The grouping of the drawings outlined above corresponds to the levels of execution of the painting, for there is a large variation in quality and finish across the surface of the panel. The areas apparently finished by Leonardo himself are those that were studied in the earlier drawings: the distant landscape, the head and shoulders of St Anne, most of the Child, the lamb's head and rear quarters, and the head-dress of the Madonna. The rest of the Madonna, for which Leonardo made his most complex studies, is painted with

the opaque waxiness typical of studio work; and the lower drapery of St Anne, the area for which we have the latest drawings, is unfinished.

Antonio de' Beatis stated, in his account of his visit to Leonardo in October 1517: "… one cannot expect any more good work from him, as a certain paralysis has crippled his right hand. But he has a pupil, a Milanese [presumably Francesco Melzi], who works well enough: and although Messer Leonardo can no longer paint with the sweetness which was peculiar to him, he can still draw and instruct others."

It has often been claimed that de' Beatis was mistaken about which of Leonardo's hands was paralysed, and that he recalled

cat. 76

cat. 77

only that it was his working hand and assumed that it was the right. But de' Beatis meant exactly what he said: Leonardo's notes and drawings, done with the left hand, were strong and confident almost to the end of his life, and it is likely that only painting and other larger-scale manual tasks that required both hands were curtailed by the paralysis in his right hand. Leonardo had continued the physically demanding practice of anatomical dissection well into his Roman period, and it may be assumed that his right hand was just as strong then. So some time between, say, 1515 and mid-1517 Leonardo lost the use of that hand, and thereafter the painting of the still unfinished *St Anne* panel was delegated to his assistants, working under his supervision and using his drawings.

136   *1508–1516: Milan and Rome*

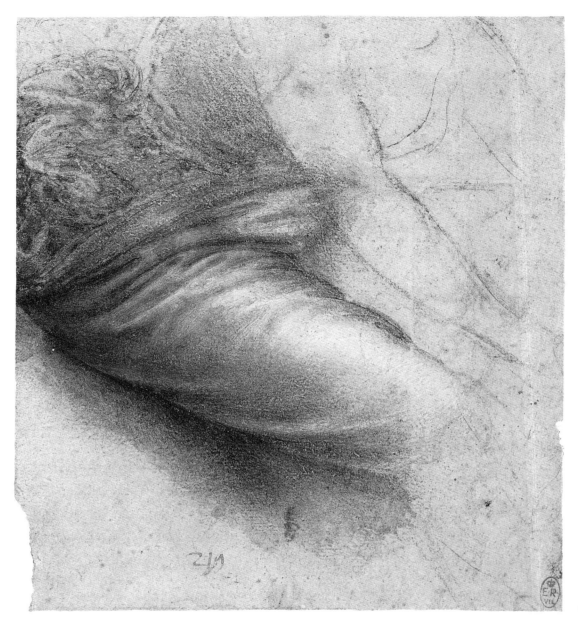

cat. 78

cat. 79

cat. 80

1517–1519
France

Leonardo had reached France by 16 January 1517, when he was at Romorantin in the Loire valley planning a canal. By May that year he had settled at the nearby palace of Amboise, where he held a privileged position as *premier peinctre et ingenieur et architecte du Roy*. Leonardo earned his keep by providing designs for entertainments, by advising on architectural and engineering matters, and generally by being an ornament to the court; some years later, Benvenuto Cellini reported Francis I as saying that he "took such pleasure in hearing [Leonardo] talk that he would only on a few days of the year deprive himself of his company". After two of the most gratifying years of his life, Leonardo died on 2 May 1519.

Information on Leonardo's activities in France is hard to come by. We know from drawings in the Codex Atlanticus that he planned several architectural projects, most spectacularly a new palace at Romorantin coupled with the canalization of the Sauldre, and that he was obsessed with geometry. Vasari (1550) stated that Leonardo went to France "to do the cartoon of the *St Anne* in colours", and as we have seen, this is probably half correct; Lomazzo (1584) wrote of a painting of *Pomona*, probably identical with the panel attributed to Francesco Melzi in the Bodemuseum, Berlin, and of anamorphic representations of horses made for the king (see cat. 95).

The most trustworthy report of Leonardo's years in France is the short account by Antonio de' Beatis of the visit of Cardinal Luigi d'Aragona to Leonardo at Amboise on 10 October 1517, already mentioned in the discussion of the *St Anne* project. As well as the *St Anne* he saw a portrait of "a certain Florentine lady" and the Louvre *St John the Baptist*. But the most important information for our purposes was that, although disabled in his right hand, Leonardo could still draw, and this is amply borne out by the number of confident drawings from this period in the Codex Atlanticus; the last dated note among Leonardo's surviving papers (C.A. f. 103r–a) shows that he still had a firm left hand in June 1518.

The drawings by Leonardo and his studio at Windsor and in the Codex Atlanticus are, on the whole, sheets left to Melzi at Leonardo's death, among which there must have been a disproportionate number from Leonardo's last years. We know of substantial losses to the manuscripts in Melzi's collection, and it is reasonable to suppose that the loose sheets also suffered losses; but since there is no evidence that these depredations were selective, significantly distorting the distribution by subject or by period of the surviving sheets, a large number of late drawings should be expected. Yet Carlo Pedretti, in an important article published in 1970, accepted only nine sheets at Windsor (from more than six hundred) as being from his French period. Is this paucity real, or a consequence of our lack of information on Leonardo's activities in France?

The recently completed conservation project at Windsor that has seen every sheet in the Leonardo group lifted from its old mount has revealed a number of French watermarks, only some of which were visible at the time of Clark and Pedretti's catalogue of 1968–69. Since these watermarks are of great importance in an analysis of Leonardo's late drawings, it is necessary to summarize them here.

1. Fleur de lys in shield, surmounted by cross with three nails: RL 12508 (cat. 89), 12577 (cat. 91). Close to Briquet 1567 (Chartres 1498), Briquet 1571 (St-Malo 1515, etc). In the range Briquet 1540–638, 255 examples, centred on northern France; none south of the Alps.

2. Bunch of grapes: RL 12342 (cat. 82), 12360 (cat. 84). Close to Briquet 13042 (Lyons 1483–84). In the range

Detail of cat. 92

Briquet 13028–43, 122 examples, mainly in France and Germany; 13 in Piedmont.

3. Orb: RL 12329, 12331 (cat. 95), 12388 (cat. 94), 12341 (fig. 18), 12793. Close to Briquet 2960 (Geneva 1529). In the range Briquet 2947–62, 47 examples, mainly in France; none south of the Alps.

4. Saddled unicorn: RL 12527 (cat. 79), 12528. Close to Briquet 10405 (Neubourg 1516), Briquet 10406 (Châteaudun 1521, La-Ferté-Aurain 1534). In the range Briquet 10378–411, 63 examples, exclusively French.

5. Catherine wheel: the most common watermark in Leonardo's late drawings, with several variants:

- simple, six-bladed: RL 12573 (cat. 88). Close to Briquet 13278 (Tours 1507, 1509), Briquet 13280 (Tours 1516–30, Clermont-Ferrand 1527).

- surmounted by three flowers: RL 12344 (cat. 83). Close to Briquet 13367 (Bourges 1512–17), Briquet 13372 (Châteaudun 1534).

- with five (not six) blades, surmounted by a crown: RL 12293. Close to Briquet 13544 (Tours 1527, Rillé 1527).

- surmounted by the letters IM (?) and a cut device: RL 12537 (the other fragment of this mark is possibly that on Codex Arundel f. 211). Not in Briquet.

- containing the letters IM and surmounted by a crown: RL 12291, 12292, 12303, 12309, 12313 (cat. 87), 12314. Close to Briquet 13565 (Rillé 1519). (The statement in Clark and Pedretti that RL 12294, cat. 26, of *ca.* 1491–92, bears a Catherine-wheel mark is erroneous.)

In the full range Briquet 13243–568, of the many hundreds of examples five are documented south of the Alps, all in Piedmont.

Watermarks are of course not a secure indication of where paper was used, for it was often traded over substantial distances; but the above analysis should demonstrate that there was no significant transalpine traffic in paper, despite the French occupation of northern Italy in the early sixteenth century – why haul paper over the Alps when there were plentiful supplies in Italy? So while Leonardo's use of one or two French papers in Italy might be explained as chance, it is wholly improbable that such a wide range was available to him before he travelled to France (and it may be noted in addition that the Catherine-wheel variants are centred on the Loire valley). It has been suggested that Leonardo may have visited France in the company of Charles d'Amboise some time around 1509 (Clark and Pedretti, under RL 12292); while this would account for some French papers in drawings of Leonardo's second Milanese period, it would not explain the many links, both of style and of motif, among the drawings listed above.

The orb watermark connects the widest range of material. Three of the drawings bearing this mark – the design for a fantastic helmet (RL 12329), the study for an equestrian monument (fig. 18) and the fragmentary half-length (RL 12793) – are among the feeblest drawings by Leonardo to survive, and they must date from the very end of his life. The other two (cats. 94, 95) are strong and decisive, and support what we know from Leonardo's dated notes, that his left hand was sound well into 1518. Among the other French-watermarked sheets, two are the *St Anne* project, as discussed above (cats. 80), and three are from the group of costume studies (cats. 88–93). But the most notable drawings here proposed as French are those hitherto associated with the Trivulzio equestrian monument.

A French equestrian monument

Many of the studies at Windsor of a horse and rider and of the detailed anatomy of the horse, in black chalk occasionally reinforced in pen and ink, are stylistically and technically distinct from the small group of studies in pen and ink alone that are certainly for the Trivulzio project (cats. 62–64). Four of the studies showing the whole horse (cats. 82–84 and fig. 18) bear French watermarks, as do seven of the detail studies; none bears an Italian mark.

One of these studies, cat. 86, had already been accepted by Clark as very late; he dissociated it from the remainder of the Trivulzio studies and suggested that it was "Leonardo's final word on a problem which had interested him all his life". Pedretti (1987) also opined that "it could even date from Leonardo's French period", while acknowledging that it was in the same style as cat. 84. The technique of this drawing – in which one side of the paper was tinted with a buff wash before being drawn on in black chalk – is also found in the series of detailed studies of the horse's anatomy (including cat. 87), and, with a slightly darker wash, in two other late drawings, a study for the *St Anne* (cat. 79) and one of the *Deluges* (see cats. 96–99). This seems to have been a technique used by Leonardo only in the last years of his life.

One of the detailed studies of horses (RL 12292) in this group has on its verso a black-chalk perspective sketch of a huge square palace with corner towers, close in form to a design for the palace of Romorantin (C.A. f. 76v–b), as noted by Heydenreich. Clark and Pedretti observed that the island setting, approached by two bridges, is rather that of Amboise, sketch-mapped by Leonardo in 1517–18 (Codex Arundel f. 269r); but in assuming that the drawing on the recto must be for the Trivulzio project, they stated that "there is no way as yet to explain Leonardo's intentions in planning such a huge palace ten years earlier than the period of his Romorantin projects". If the horse study on the recto is instead dated ten years later, this difficulty disappears.

A good copy of one of the 'Trivulzio' drawings is on a sheet in the Codex Atlanticus (f. 290v–b); this sheet has been dated to 1508–10 primarily because of the presence of a 'Trivulzio' horse, but the pupil's drawing of a profile on the same sheet may be compared with that on C.A. f. 88r–a, a sheet of 1517–18, and the geometrical study of a pyramid on the other side of the sheet recurs in a similar form on C.A. f. 335v–e, also probably of the French period.

The only significant obstacle to this proposed split of the 'Trivulzio' drawings is the sheet RL 12356. On its recto is a drawing in red chalk of the whole monument (fig. 16), with the horse and rider worked over in pen and ink; the architecture is very similar to the study at the lower right of cat. 64, and the technique and style are closely comparable with some of the water studies of around 1510 (cats. 65, 66). This drawing is the only study for the Trivulzio monument in which the horse is shown walking, apart from the marginal sketch on the sheet of notes on casting (RL 12347). On the verso of RL 12356 is a study in nebulous black chalk, inked in around the outline of the horse, the inking being a tracing of the horse on the recto; but the verso drawing is stylistically inseparable from several of the drawings here proposed as from the French period, notably cats. 85 and 92.

This stylistic dilemma can only be resolved by suggesting that some ten years elapsed between the execution of the two sides of the sheet. Although there are few instances of Leonardo reusing a sheet after a gap of several years, this is not improbable here; he had the Trivulzio drawings with him in France, and would doubtless have referred to them when working on a late equestrian project; why should he not draw on the back of one of them?

It must be emphasized that there is no document to support this theory of a French equestrian project, but this is only one document less than the sum of our knowledge of the Trivulzio project. It is possible that after the stroke that affected his right side, Leonardo realised that he could not execute the putative monument; he does not appear to have put his mind seriously to the practicalities of casting. It is also pure speculation to attempt to identify the person honoured, other than to make the obvious guess that it was the King (either Louis or Francis), for Leonardo was not one for portraiture in his sculptural sketches, and no heraldic emblem is depicted.

A bronze statuette in Budapest, similar in pose to cat. 86, has often been claimed to be by Leonardo, usually of the time of the *Battle* of *Anghiari* (*ca.* 1504–06), but Agghàzy (1989) argued that it was made for Francis I in Leonardo's French period. It is impossible to be insistent about the authorship of such a sculpture when we have nothing to compare it with, and the mass of peripheral information about the court of Francis I marshalled by Agghàzy ultimately proves nothing. But an attribution to Leonardo of the Budapest sculpture is stylistically plausible, and although the anatomy of the horse does not seem worthy of a lifetime's study by the master, it may reflect an original by him. In the absence of any documentary evidence of a full-scale equestrian monument in Leonardo's French period, it is possible that his dreams of a rearing horse in bronze were finally realised, not without bathos, in a statuette.

81

Studies for an equestrian monument

ca. 1517–18
Black chalk
267 x 161 mm (10½″ x 6⁵⁄₁₆″)
No watermark
RL 12359

82

Studies for an equestrian monument

ca. 1517–18
Black chalk
278 x 184 mm (10¹⁵⁄₁₆″ x 7¼″)
Watermark: bunch of grapes (cut), close to Briquet 13042
RL 12342

83

Studies for an equestrian monument

ca. 1517–18
Black chalk, pen and ink
203 x 143 mm (8″ x 5⅝″)
Watermark: Catherine wheel surmounted by three flowers, close to Briquet 13367, 13372
RL 12344

84

Studies for an equestrian monument

ca. 1517–18
Black chalk, some pen and ink
224 x 160 mm (8¹³⁄₁₆″ x 6⁵⁄₁₆″)
Watermark: as cat. 82 (probably two portions of the same sheet)
RL 12360

85

A study for an equestrian monument

ca. 1517–18
Black chalk, pen and ink
153 x 144 mm (6″ x 5¹¹⁄₁₆″)
No watermark
RL 12343

86

A study for an equestrian monument

ca. 1517–18
Black chalk on paper washed pale buff
201 x 124 mm (7¹⁵⁄₁₆″ x 4⅞″)
No watermark
RL 12354

87

Studies of a horse

ca. 1517–18
Black-chalk underdrawing, pen and ink on
paper washed pale buff
203 x 158 mm (8″ x 6¼″)
Watermark: Catherine wheel containing
letters IM and surmounted by a crown (cut),
close to Briquet 13565
RL 12313

The upper horse in cat. 81 is unusual among Leonardo's equestrian studies in moving with an ambling gait, both legs on the same side advanced, an unnatural movement for which horses must be trained. This is the gait of the major equestrian monuments of the fifteenth century – Donatello's *Gattamelata*, Verrocchio's *Colleoni*, and the frescos of Uccello and Castagno in Florence Cathedral – and would have indicated to a contemporary spectator, much more aware of horsemanship than we are, the qualities of culture and control. But it had the practical drawback in a sculpture of requiring the advanced rear leg to be firmly grounded to stabilize the monument, and elsewhere Leonardo prefers the slightly more high-stepping natural walk, as at the centre of cat. 81. These two gaits, ambling and walking, are discussed by Leonardo in a note on RL 12303.

The lower study of cat. 81 is one of Leonardo's most elegant solutions to the material problem of the monument. Most of the weight is taken on the rear legs as the rider reins in the horse, while the poses of both move both backwards

cat. 81

cat. 82

cat. 83

121

cat. 84

Fig. 18
Leonardo da Vinci
Studies of a horse for an equestrian monument
Black chalk, 122 x 175 mm (4¹³⁄₁₆″ x 6⅞″)
RL 12341

in actuality and forwards in intent. The geometrical diagram to upper right is not connected with the monument: it is one of countless lunulae, geometrical studies of segments of circles, that are found throughout Leonardo's late manuscripts, and could indicate any date in the last ten years or so of his life.

The lower of the two large studies in cat. 82 attempts to capture something of the duality of the lower drawing in cat. 81, with the rider looking backwards while gesturing forwards, but the horse is here unresponsive to his movements. In both main drawings the rider is shown with the shimmering cloak of the late masquerade studies (cats. 88–93), and the upper figure appears to be wearing a laurel wreath. This study was drawn in two stages: a lighter sketch of horse and rider with the horse's head dropped was revised by strengthening the outlines of the horse and raising its head.

Cat. 83 shows the horse in profile again, in a delicate pen-and-ink crystallization of a vaporous sketch as Leonardo manipulated the proportions in black chalk. The two drawings below are the only studies for the monument (excluding the studies of anatomy) that show the body in anything other than profile. They examine the effects of twisting the head first in the direction of the raised foreleg, then in opposition to it. The edges of the plinth are drawn, but no other architecture is indicated.

Cat. 84 contains the most resolved of the late equestrian studies, in the carefully finished drawing at lower left. Here Leonardo pays some attention to the architectural support of the monument, a relatively low plinth with a tablet flanked

cat. 85

by two pilasters – another reason to dissociate these studies from the Trivulzio project, where the equestrian group had to be combined with a setting for a sarcophagus. The horse's raised legs are supported by the contrivances of a tortoise (symbol of patience and constancy) and a pouring ewer (bounty), more appropriate to a monarch than to a military leader.

The two central studies return to the motif of the rearing horse, which Leonardo first proposed for the Sforza monument before surrendering to the technical difficulties, then revived for the Trivulzio monument, again reverting to the walking pose. Here at the end of his life he rekindled his ambition of creating an equestrian monument of drama and dynamism – the triumph of hope over experience. It was over a century before the practical problems of a full-scale rearing horse in bronze were solved, in Pietro Tacca's monument to Philip IV of Spain, and then partly by virtue of a fashion for long tails that allowed the sculptor a substantial counterweight to the free front half of the horse.

Cat. 85 is among the latest of the equestrian studies. The penwork has the cursory, even careless assurance of drawings such as the costume study, cat. 93. The pose of the horse is that of fig. 18, a very late drawing in which Leonardo has lost something of his power of hand, and the horse's head of cat. 85 is identical to the separate detail on that sheet. The rider is wearing contemporary armour, akin to the Trivulzio study (fig. 16), but the horse is more powerfully built here than in perhaps any other equestrian study by Leonardo.

Cat. 86 appears distinct in conception from the other late equestrian studies, although the technique is that of the detail sheets such as cat. 87, and the style is indistinguishable from that of cat. 84.

cat. 86

The pose of the fallen soldier is hard to discern; he appears to be kneeling forwards, left leg sticking out behind, while twisting round violently to the right, pushing up the horse's chest with his right arm and its off foreleg with his left.

The architecture is more elaborate than that shown in any of the other late studies. A vaguely indicated trophy seems to be at the centre of the heavy entablature, which rests on two groups of pilasters enclosing niches; below these are the beginnings of another order of members, lost when the sheet was trimmed. Pedretti (1987) suggested that the group might be for a monumental portal, but in that case either the door would be impractically narrow or the monument impossibly large. An alternative suggestion of a monumental arch would also leave the architecture looking puny beneath the massive horse, and it may be that the members were sketched in by Leonardo merely to give some context to the horse, without considering the proportions of the monument as a whole.

Cat. 87 is one of a number of drawings in black chalk, often worked up in pen and ink, on paper washed pale buff on one side, that study the superficial anatomy of the horse in some detail. A stylistic case could be made to date the drawings to any time after about 1510, on the basis of their soft black chalk and tight, curving pen-lines found from the time of Anatomical MS. A (cats. 67–69) until the end of Leonardo's life (cats. 93, 94). But, as discussed above, all are on French paper; the method of washing the paper buff is that of cats. 79 and 86; and one sheet (RL 12292) bears on its verso a study for one of the architectural projects that occupied Leonardo during his last years at the French court.

cat. 87

cat. 88

Costume studies

88

A masquerader in the guise of a prisoner

ca. 1517–18
Black chalk, with some red-chalk offsetting
184 x 127 mm (7¼″ x 5″)
Watermark: six-bladed Catherine wheel, close
to Briquet 13278, 13280
RL 12573

89

A study for the costume of a masquerader, in profile

ca. 1517–18
Black chalk, with some red-chalk offsetting
170 x 146 mm (6¹¹⁄₁₆″ x 5¾″)
Watermark: fleur de lys in shield surmounted
by cross with three nails, close to Briquet
1567, 1571
RL 12508

90

A study for the costume of a masquerader

ca. 1517–18
Black chalk
215 x 112 mm (8⁷⁄₁₆″ x 4⁷⁄₁₆″)
No watermark
RL 12576

91

A study for the costume of a masquerader

ca. 1517–18
Black chalk
214 x 107 mm (8⁷⁄₁₆″ x 4³⁄₁₆″)
Watermark: as cat. 89
RL 12577

92

*A study of a dragon costume for
an entertainment*

ca. 1517–18
Black chalk, pen and ink
188 x 270 mm (7⅜″ x 10⅝″)
Watermark: letter A in circle surmounted by
letter P, close to Briquet 9608
RL 12369

93

*A study for the costume of a
masquerader on horseback*

ca. 1517–18
Black-chalk underdrawing, pen and ink
240 x 152 mm (9⁷⁄₁₆″ x 6″)
No watermark
RL 12574

Feasts, dances, tournaments and mock
battles were a staple of courtly life across
Europe in the fifteenth and sixteenth centuries. They provided diversions for the
restive nobility, and allowed a ruler to play
host to foreign dignitaries, ostensibly
entertaining them while simultaneously
impressing them with the sophistication
and ingenuity of his resources – and often

cat. 90

the same individuals, like Leonardo, would design machines for amusement and for war. Major artists devoted much time and effort to settings and costumes for these important occasions, and the total absence of any visual record of many of them is a serious lacuna in our understanding of the period.

A few costume studies by Leonardo do survive at Windsor, and some rough stage designs elsewhere, though they must be a tiny fraction of the designs made in his capacity as a court artist throughout his life – first in Sforza Milan, then under the French occupiers of the same city, in the entourage of Giuliano de' Medici, and finally at the French court in the Loire valley. Some of the events for which Leonardo may have provided designs are documented, and probably all of them have been claimed at one time or another as the occasions for which he produced the extant drawings. No costume design matches a contemporary description exactly, but the style and paper of cats. 88–93 point decisively to their production in the last years of Leonardo's life, at the French court.

Cats. 88–91 appear to have been drawn at the same time. On the verso of cat. 88 is an aborted underdrawing for the legs and torso of a figure in the vigorous pose of cats. 90 and 91 (an echo of Verrocchio's bronze *David*, probably executed when Leonardo was in the sculptor's studio more than forty years earlier), and cat. 89 bears a French watermark identical to that on cat. 91. As Clark noted, "the dress and accoutrements of the prisoner are almost too picturesque" for cat. 88 to represent a real captive (who would hardly carry a club), and the elaborate layers of ragged clothing were no doubt intended as a foil to the bundles of flowing ribbons and diaphanous drapery of cats. 89–91.

The hairstyles of cats. 89 and 90 are identical (although the masqueraders appear to be female and male respectively), wound around the head and knotted with a tail emerging from the knot, and dressed at the front into a shell-like crest. In concept these are closer to the *coiffures* of Michelangelo's ideal heads than to Leonardo's earlier designs such as the wig worn by Leda (cat. 40). The handling of the black chalk in all four, though more precise in cat. 88, is very close to that of the late equestrian studies, cats. 81–87.

Cat. 92 is rather harder to place. Clark and Pedretti had already accepted a date close to that of the black chalk masquerade studies (although they placed these around 1512–13), and supported a proposal that the dragon was an illustration to Dante. The similarity to Dante's description (*Inferno*, XXV, 50–51) is not close enough to warrant this identification; the proportions, and particularly the manner in which the body and legs are articulated, support instead a later suggestion that the drawing is a design for a costume to house two performers, in the manner of a pantomime horse. It is so similar in style to the other masquerade drawings, and to some of the late equestrian studies (especially cat. 85 and RL 12356v), that it is surely of the French period; however, it does bear an Italian watermark – this would be the only instance of a French-period drawing on Italian paper, implying that Leonardo did not carry much unused paper with him to France.

Cat. 93 is technically distinct from the other costume drawings shown here, though it is stylistically identical to cat. 94, and must also date from the last years of Leonardo's life. It is on the same porridgy paper as another costume study, RL 12575, and is presumably for the same masque, but there is no compelling

cat. 91

cat.

reason to suppose that they were for the same entertainment as cats. 88–92.

Pedretti connected cat. 93 and RL 12575 with the costumes worn during the pageant to honour the visit of Pope Leo X to Florence in 1515, as described by Landucci: "... about fifty youths ... all dressed in a livery of clothing of peacock-blue fabric with squirrel-fur at the neck, on foot, with little silvered lances in their hands – a very beautiful thing; and then the greatest parade of cavalry ...."

With the exception of the lances, this does not tally at all closely with either cat. 93 or RL 12575, and a better character-ization of the elaborate nature of cats. 88–93 is perhaps provided by descriptions

of the entertainments held by Francis I at Amboise and Romorantin during January 1518 for the young Federico Gonzaga of Mantua, then completing his education at the French court. The events are re-counted in a number of surviving letters written by the Mantuan secretary, Stazio Gadio (see Shearman 1978); for instance at one he described Federico as: "... very showy, dressed as a lansquenet, with half-boots, one completely dark, the other less dark, edged with a white and yellow rib-and cut in the German manner, a tunic half of satin, the edge of silver cloth, and golden cloth made into scales, with a German-style shirt worked with gold, and over this a cape of dark cloth fitted

with a riband of gold and silver cloth made in the French manner ...."

There is not a precise match with any of Leonardo's surviving designs, but the lavishness and concern with layering is exactly as found in the drawings, and we may assume, given Leonardo's position at the court, that he provided drawings for these costumes. Cats. 88–93 are probably designs for unrecorded costumes at other entertainments, of which there were many at the court of the young Francis I, including in May 1518 the festivities to celebrate the wedding of Madeleine de La Tour d'Auvergne to Lorenzo di Piero de' Medici, Leonardo's patron three years earlier in Florence.

cat. 93

94

Scenes of Apocalypse and Resurrection

ca. 1518
Black-chalk underdrawing, pen and ink, on coarse paper
300 x 203 mm (11¹³⁄₁₆″ x 8″)
Watermark: orb, close to Briquet 2960
RL 12388

The four separate sketches here show scenes from the end of the world: above, fire rains from heaven, burning up tiny figures as a fortress crumbles to the left; to the lower right, more mannekins are incinerated; a great ball of smoke and fire burns over mountains and a boiling sea at lower centre; to the left, skeletons climb from their graves. The notes on the sheet are, by contrast, coolly scientific, discussing the appearance of clouds (of rain, dust or smoke) when lit by the sun – a subject that interested Leonardo deeply during the last few years of his career, as he continued to compile material for his intended treatise on painting. A very similar note is found on RL 12391, certainly datable to the end of Leonardo's life; the present drawing is on French paper with the orb watermark and must also date from these years (see pp. 140–41).

Many possible sources for the images illustrated here have been suggested: the Books of Ezekiel, Matthew or Revelation, the writings of Seneca, even reports of a natural disaster that befell Lombardy in 1513; but a faithful illustration of a text – in particular a religious text – would be out of character for Leonardo at any point of his career, and especially so towards the end of his life, when he had accumulated such a rich personal iconography of catastrophe and destruction that he would have had no need to follow another's writings. The present drawings are thus probably best interpreted as nothing more nor less than an effusion of Leonardo's fertile imagination.

Two details of cat. 94

95

Sketches of horses, a lioness, and a dragon fight

ca. 1517–18
Black-chalk underdrawing, pen and ink, wash,
on coarse paper
298 x 212 mm (11¾″ x 8⅜″), upper edge
tattered
Watermark: as cat. 94
RL 12331

This sheet has been associated with a projected treatise on the movement of animals: "Write a separate treatise describing
the movements of animals with four feet,
among which is man, who likewise in his
infancy crawls on all fours" (MS. E, f. 16r,
ca. 1513–14). Although Leonardo never
pursued the subject in any systematic or
sustained way, he was particularly interested towards the end of his life in the
flexible spine of animals, and wrote at the
top of this page: *The serpentine nature of the
postures is the principal action in the movement
of animals.*

Leonardo thus assembles horses, a
lioness, and five groups of a rider on
horseback (possibly St George) slaying a
dragon, each displaying strong twists to
the back and neck. The only horse not
contorted is that at lower left, walking in
a pose very similar to several of the late
equestrian studies; and the St George at
upper right is strikingly close to the study
for a monument atop a portal, cat. 86.
The sheet bears the orb watermark, in
common with RL 12329, which also
features a peculiarly twisted horse (and
a helmet for a masquerade) and must be
one of Leonardo's latest drawings, when
he was losing power in his left hand as
well as in his right. All the evidence
points to the present sheet being of Leonardo's French period, and the sheet may
possibly be related to the anamorphic
depictions of horses described by
Lomazzo (*Trattato*, p. 335f.) as made for
Francis I.

Two details of cat. 95

cat. 9[...]

Deluges

96

A deluge

ca. 1517–18
Black chalk
158 x 210 mm (6¼″ x 8¼″)
No watermark
RL 12385

97

A deluge

ca. 1517–18
Black chalk
161 x 207 mm (6⅜″ x 8⅛″)
No watermark
RL 12382

98

A deluge

ca. 1517–18
Black chalk
165 x 204 mm (6½″ x 8¹⁄₁₆″)
No watermark
RL 12384

99

A deluge

ca. 1517–18
Black chalk
158 x 210 mm (6¼″ x 8¼″)
No watermark
RL 12383

These four sheets belong to a series of eleven drawings of a mighty deluge at Windsor (RL 12377–86, 12401), uniform in size and style but not in technique, which is one of the most enigmatic products of Leonardo's career. Leonardo was much taken with describing scenes of cataclysm towards the end of his life, and

although there exist several long passages where he recounts with relish the futile struggling of man and animal against the overwhelming forces of nature, there is no direct, illustrative relationship between any of these descriptions and the *Deluge* drawings. Attempts have been made to arrange them as a sequence, but other than the differing degrees of chaos there seems little basis for any such reconstruction; similarly a proposal that the so called *Pointing lady in a landscape* (RL 12581) is an introductory sheet to the series (on whatever level) is rather forced. Nonetheless some of the drawings are connected in scale and motif, and the four shown here can be strung together as a narrative – though not necessarily the correct one.

In cat. 96, the storm breaks over a large town, sending water cascading over the city walls and down the surrounding hills, washing away trees and fences. A mountain fortress to the lower right is powerless to defend itself against the torrents. Cat. 97 shows the town torn apart by the huge swirls of water descending from above; the flood has inundated the countryside, and the fortress has disintegrated, its walls collapsing outwards and down the slopes of the mountain. In cat. 98 the winds change direction, sweeping up the valley to lift the debris into the air, which is rent by bolts of lightning visible through the rain, dust and smoke. Cat. 99 shows the destruction complete, with nothing solid remaining, just great plumes of water issuing from the looming clouds on to the drowned landscape below.

The date of the series is uncertain. RL 12376, a *Deluge* drawing which is not *en suite* with RL 12377–86 (being twice the size) but which bears strong similarities to the whole series, was dated after 1516 by Pedretti (1982), who compared both style and technique to sheets securely of Leonardo's French period. A note referring to Francis I's military expedition in Italy in 1515, on a page carrying a description of a deluge (C.A. f. 79r–c), might provide a *terminus post quem* for the series of drawings, albeit not a very reliable one. None of the sheets bears a watermark.

Another clue might be provided by RL 12381, which has been described as a copy on account of its perceived 'uncertain' touch. It is on the same buff-washed paper as cat. 79, one of the last studies for the *St Anne*; indeed it is washed to exactly the same tone on the recto, and the handling of the chalk is identical. Cat. 79 is certainly by Leonardo; the apparent difference in touch between RL 12381 and the rest of the *Deluge* series is a consequence of the wash preparation of the paper, which has changed the surface texture and with it the character of the chalk strokes. Thus it becomes possible to date RL 12381 to *ca.* 1517–18; and if it is assumed that the whole *Deluge* series is contemporary, they must all be of Leonardo's French period.

Some support for this dating is found in the only extraneous material on any

of the sheets, a discordantly calm note on RL 12380 about optical effects in rainfall, analogous to cat. 94 of *ca.* 1518 where apocalyptic scenes are accompanied by a note on the fall of light on clouds. The conjunction of scientific notes and chaotic drawings on several sheets from Leonardo's last years is not as odd as it might appear, for the notes were not independent studies in meteorology but were conceived as passages towards Leonardo's treatise on painting, to help the artist depict such atmospheric effects.

The function of the series of drawings has never been explained satisfactorily. The verso of each one is blank, and although the sheets have been cut down, framing lines are visible along some of the edges. This, and the uniformity of size, strongly suggests that the series was intended as an independent work of art, but as the drawings came to Windsor from the Melzi/Leoni collection, they presumably never left Leonardo's studio. The problem perhaps lies in our attempts to understand Leonardo's creative processes in terms of those of other artists. In his last years in France, an adornment to the court with a secure living and an appreciative patron, Leonardo could indulge many of his fantasies and interests without the need to produce something saleable or presentable, and the *Deluge* series may simply have been made for his own satisfaction.

100

Copy after Leonardo
A portrait of Leonardo

ca. 1520 (?)
Red chalk
275 x 190 mm (10¹³/₁₆″ x 7½″), corners cut
No watermark
RL 12726

Although not by Leonardo, this drawing is of high quality and is probably a faithful copy of a lost self-portrait from the later years of his life: the head is seen from a conspicuously close viewpoint, as would result from an artist using an angled pair of small mirrors to study his own profile. Unusually for a drawing from the Melzi/Leoni collection, cat. 100 has been shaped for mounting, and is in relatively poor condition; indeed it shows signs of having been stuck on to a support, lifted and restored at an early date. It was presumably a valued memento of the master, and it is therefore possible that this is the portrait seen by Vasari in the villa of Francesco Melzi, who inherited Leonardo's manuscripts: "Francesco cherishes and preserves these papers as relics of Leonardo, together with the portrait of that artist of such happy memory."

The features correspond generally to every image we have of Leonardo, though the head does not have the romantically distressed qualities of the much more famous self-portrait drawing in Turin (fig. 19). The Turin sheet is an intermediate between the objectivity of cat. 100 and the many caricatures of wizened old men found in Leonardo's later drawings; there the face has none of the equanimity of cat. 100, and the furrowed brow and narrowed eyes may be read as the expression of private visions or thwarted ambition – or both.

Fig. 19 Leonardo da Vinci, *Self-portrait*
Red chalk, 333 x 214 mm (13⅛″ x 8⁷/₁₆″). Turin, Biblioteca Reale

Further reading

All the drawings at Windsor were catalogued and reproduced in K. Clark and C. Pedretti, *The Drawings of Leonardo da Vinci in the Collection of Her Majesty The Queen at Windsor Castle*, 3 vols., London 1968–69. The first three parts of a projected series of facsimiles of the Windsor drawings have also been published:

K. Keele and C. Pedretti, *Leonardo da Vinci: Corpus of the Anatomical Studies in the Collection of Her Majesty The Queen at Windsor Castle*, 2 vols. and facsimiles, London and New York 1979

C. Pedretti, *The Drawings and Miscellaneous Papers of Leonardo da Vinci in the Collection of Her Majesty The Queen at Windsor Castle. Vol. I: Landscapes, Plants and Water Studies*, London and New York 1982 (a partial version of this text is available in *Leonardo da Vinci: Nature Studies …*, exh. cat., London, Royal Academy, etc, 1981)

Idem, Vol. II: Horses and Other Animals, London and New York 1987 (a partial version of this text is available in *Leonardo's Horses …*, exh. cat., Florence, Palazzo Vecchio, 1984, and *Leonardo da Vinci: Drawings of Horses …*, exh. cat., Washington, National Gallery of Art, etc, 1985)

The other major collection of Leonardo's drawings, the Codex Atlanticus in the Biblioteca Ambrosiana, Milan, has been published twice in facsimile, more recently as *Il Codice Atlantico di Leonardo da Vinci*, 12 vols., Florence 1973–75, with a transcription in a further 12 vols. by A. Marinoni (Florence 1975) and an independent catalogue in 2 vols. by C. Pedretti, London and New York 1978. All of Leonardo's notebooks have also been published in facsimile, for which refer to a more comprehensive bibliography. The best compendium of Leonardo's writings is J.P. Richter, *The Literary Works of Leonardo da Vinci*, 3rd edn., 2 vols., London and New York 1970, which should be read in conjunction with C. Pedretti, *The Literary Works of Leonardo da Vinci: A Commentary to Jean Paul Richter's Edition*, Oxford 1977. The most coherent reconstruction of Leonardo's planned treatise is *Leonardo on Painting*, ed. and trans. M. Kemp and M. Walker, New Haven and London 1989.

The most complete catalogue of Leonardo's drawings from all collections is A.E. Popham, *The Drawings of Leonardo da Vinci*, London 1946 (and later editions). As a general introduction to Leonardo's life and works, K. Clark, *Leonardo da Vinci, An Account of his Development as an Artist*, Cambridge 1939 (and later editions) remains unsurpassed.

There follows a highly selective list of some of the works that the author found useful in compiling the present catalogue:

M.G. Agghàzy, *Leonardo's Equestrian Statuette*, Budapest 1989

B. Barryte, 'The "Ill-Matched Couple"', *Achademia Leonardi Vinci*, III, 1990, pp. 133–39

L. Beltrami, *Documenti e memorie riguardanti la vita e le opere di Leonardo da Vinci*, Milan 1919

G. Calvi, *I manoscritti di Leonardo da Vinci dal punto di vista cronologico, storico e biografico*, Bologna 1925; ed. A. Marinoni, Busto Arsizio 1982

M. Clayton and R. Philo, *Leonardo da Vinci: The Anatomy of Man*, exh. cat., Houston, Museum of Fine Arts, 1992

W. Emboden, *Leonardo da Vinci on Plants and Gardens*, Portland 1987

J. Fletcher, 'Bernardo Bembo and Leonardo's *Portrait of Ginevra de Benci*', *Burlington Magazine*, CXXXI, 1989, pp. 811–16

L. Fusco and G. Corti, 'Lorenzo de' Medici on the Sforza Monument', *Achademia Leonardi Vinci*, V, 1992, pp. 11–32

C. Gould, *Leonardo: The Artist and the Non-Artist*, London 1975

L. Heydenreich, 'Leonardo da Vinci, Architect of Francis I', *Burlington Magazine*, XCIV, 1952, pp. 277–85

P. Joannides, 'Leonardo da Vinci, Peter-Paul Rubens, Pierre-Nolasque Bergeret and the "Fight for the Standard"', *Achademia Leonardi Vinci*, I, 1988, pp. 76–86

K. Keele, *Leonardo da Vinci on the Movements of the Heart and Blood*, London 1952

K. Keele, *Leonardo da Vinci's Elements of the Science of Man*, New York and London 1983

M. Kemp, *Leonardo da Vinci: The Marvellous Works of Nature and Man*, London 1981

S. Kish, 'Leonardo da Vinci: The Mapmaker', in *Imago et mensura mundi. Atti del IX congresso internazionale di storia della cartografia*, Roma, Istituto dell'Enciclopedia Italiana, 1985, vol. I, pp. 89–98

M. Kwakkelstein, *Leonardo da Vinci as a Physiognomist*, Leiden 1995

Leonardo's Legacy: A Symposium, ed. C. O'Malley, Los Angeles 1969

The Unknown Leonardo, ed. L. Reti, London 1974

Leonardo da Vinci, Engineer and Architect, ed. P. Galluzzi, Montreal 1987

Leonardo da Vinci, exh. cat. by M. Kemp, J. Roberts *et al.*, London, Hayward Gallery, 1989

Leonardo da Vinci: The Mystery of the Madonna of the Yarnwinder, exh. cat. by M. Kemp *et al.*, Edinburgh, National Gallery of Scotland, 1992

Leonardo and Venice, exh. cat., Venice, Palazzo Grassi, 1992

Leonardo artista delle macchine e cartografo, ed. R. Campioni, exh. cat., Imola, Chiostri di San Domenico, 1994

F. Mancini, *Urbanistica rinascimentale a Imola da Girolamo Riario a Leonardo da Vinci*, 2 vols., Imola 1979

P. Marani, *L'architettura fortificata negli studi di Leonardo da Vinci*, Florence 1984

P. Marani, *Leonardo da Vinci*, Milan 1994

A. Marinoni, *I rebus di Leonardo da Vinci*, Florence 1954

C.D. O'Malley and J. Saunders, *Leonardo da Vinci on the Human Body*, New York 1952

C. Pedretti, 'Leonardo da Vinci: Manuscripts and drawings of the French period, 1517–1518', *Gazette des Beaux-Arts*, LXXVI, 1970, pp. 285–318

C. Pedretti, *Leonardo da Vinci: The Royal Palace at Romorantin*, Cambridge MA 1972

C. Pedretti, *Leonardo: Architect*, London 1986

C. Pedretti, 'The Angel in the Flesh', *Achademia Leonardi Vinci*, IV, 1991, pp. 34–48

R.V. Schofield, 'Leonardo's Milanese Architecture: Career, Sources and Graphic Techniques', *Achademia Leonardi Vinci*, IV, 1991, pp. 111–57

J. Shearman, 'The Galerie François Premier: A Case in Point', *Miscellanea Musicologica (Adelaide Studies in Musicology)*, II, 1978, pp. 1–16

J. Shell and G. Sironi, 'Salaì and Leonardo's Legacy', *Burlington Magazine*, CXXXIII, 1991, pp. 95–108

J. Snow-Smith, *The Salvator Mundi of Leonardo da Vinci*, Seattle 1982

E.M. Todd, *The Neuroanatomy of Leonardo da Vinci*, New York 1978

A.R. Turner, *Inventing Leonardo*, New York 1993

K. Veltman, *Studies on Leonardo da Vinci I: Linear Perspective and the Visual Dimensions of Science and Art*, Munich 1986

J. Wasserman, 'A Re-Discovered Cartoon by Leonardo da Vinci', *Burlington Magazine*, CXII, 1970, pp. 194–210

J. Wasserman, 'The Dating and Patronage of Leonardo's Burlington House Cartoon', *Art Bulletin*, LIII, 1971, pp. 312–25

E. Winternitz, *Leonardo as a Musician*, New Haven 1982

V. Zubov, *Leonardo da Vinci*, trans. D. Kraus, Cambridge MA 1968

Concordance
between Royal Library inventory numbers and catalogue entries

RL	cat.	RL	cat.	RL	cat.	RL	cat.
		12354	86	12527	79	12660	66
12276v	5	12355	64	12530	78	12661	65
12277	51	12358	23	12533	76	12677	56
12278	52	12359	81	12538	75	12678	57
12279	55	12360	84	12540	34	12683	53
12282A	28	12362	8	12546	31	12684	74
12284	50	12369	92	12547	29	12685	54
12290	25	12372	22	12551	30	12686	49
12294	26	12382	97	12554	60	12692v	13
12313	87	12383	99	12556	61	12701	59
12315	9	12384	98	12558	1	12726	100
12317	24	12385	96	12569	4	19002	69
12324	6	12388	94	12572	2	19003v	67
12325	7	12397	77	12573	88	19013v	68
12327	38	12419	42	12574	93	19032v	46
12328	39	12431v	33	12576	90	19040	47
12331	95	12424	41	12577	91	19051v	48
12334	37	12449	15	12591	58	19058v	21
12339	35	12490	14	12601	18	19059	20
12340	36	12508	89	12604	16	19071	70
12342	82	12513	3	12613v	17	19075v	73
12343	85	12514	32	12637	19	19101	71
12344	83	12518	40	12640	45	19107v	72
12349	27	12524	44	12649	12		
12353	63	12525	43	12652	11		
12353A	62	12526	80	12653	10		

Index